OTHER BOOKS BY BERNARD BAILYN

The Ordeal of Thomas Hutchinson
The Origin of American Politics
The Ideological Origins of the American Revolution
Pamphlets of the American Revolution (editor, with J. N. Garrett)
Education in the Forming of American Society
Massachusetts Shipping, 1697–1714 (with Lotte Bailyn)
The New England Merchants in the Seventeenth Century

The Peopling
of British
North
America

AN

INTRODUCTION

THE CURTI LECTURES
THE UNIVERSITY OF WISCONSIN
MCMLXXXV

The Peopling of British North America,

AN INTRODUCTION

Bernard Bailyn

MDCCCC LXXXVI

ALFRED · A · KNOPF   NEW YORK

Library of Congress Cataloging-in-Publication Data
Bailyn, Bernard.   The peopling
of British North America: an introduction.
Includes index.
1. United States—History—Colonial period,
ca. 1600–1775—Addresses, essays, lectures.   I. Title.
E188.5.B34   1986   973.2   85–82144
ISBN 0–394–55392–6
Manufactured in the United States of America
Published June 3, 1986
Second Printing, October 1986

Contents

Preface

In their original form these three essays were a single paper, written in 1978 as an effort to organize my thoughts after three years of work on a project I have called "The Peopling of British North America." A great deal of information had been gathered since I had begun the research on the early history of the American population, and I felt the need to define the questions, sketch some of the main themes, and organize the voluminous material that had come to hand. By then a large book was being planned, tracing in detail the origins and destinies of some ten thousand British emigrants to America in the years just before the Revolution (*Voyagers to the West*, Knopf, 1986); and the general work, to appear in several forms, was beginning to take shape. But I continued to revise and expand that initial short sketch of 1978, an interpretative survey of the then available writings, amplified it with borrowings from *Voyagers,* and formed it into an introduction to the overall project. When opportunities arose to present parts of the sketch to various audiences —especially at the universities of Washington and Wisconsin, and at Washington University, St. Louis—further refinements were made and new points were added. The fullest version was that of the Curti Lectures at the University of Wisconsin, and it is largely in that form that the essays are now published.

Yet, despite all of this expanding, reworking, and revising—much of it to accommodate the wealth of new writings on early American social history that has appeared over the past few years—this sketch remains essentially what it was at the start, a preliminary effort to open up the questions and identify major themes of a very large area of history which we still only vaguely understand. In time some, at least, of the story will be filled in. *Voyagers to the West*, to appear almost simultaneously with this little book, is the first substantive volume; others, I hope, will be published in subsequent years.

The general project to which the pages that follow form an introduction was made possible by matching grants from the Rockefeller Brothers Fund and the National Endowment for the Humanities (RO–0444–77) and by the generous cooperation of the Faculty of Arts and Sciences of Harvard University. I was encouraged to seek the grants by Elizabeth McCormack, for whose enthusiasm, confidence, and assistance I am deeply grateful. One day I hope her optimism, and the encouragement of Mr. William Dietel, will be justified, at least in part. And I am grateful, too, to Barbara DeWolfe. As I have explained in greater detail in the Preface to *Voyagers*, she joined me in the research at the start and has continued to the present, now as a virtual collaborator. Without her zestful burrowing in the dreariest archives, her skills with both computers and bibliographies, her sharp criticism of every page I wrote, and her marvelous good cheer, this sketch would have been far more defective than it is.

B. B.

I

Worlds in Motion

I would like to introduce my subject with a flight of fancy. I would like to imagine a satellite circling the globe from the early medieval period to the advent of industrialism, equipped with a camera of perfect accuracy, a camera capable of scanning vast areas in a single sweep and yet of focusing on the smallest region or community at any point of time. I want to imagine that this circling eye could bring together into a single view groups, individuals, and places scattered over hundreds, even thousands, of miles and over decades, even centuries of time, and that it could catch not only the outward appearance of people, their physical movements, and their palpable way of life, but also their interior experiences, the quality of their culture, the capacity of their minds, the patterns of their emotions.

With such a camera, one could grasp the essence of historical change, the evanescence that is the heart and soul of history, and the elusive ambiguity of historical movement. But what, from that vantage point, would impress one as the most sweeping and striking development in this millennium of Western history? The most visible physically, I think, would be deforestation and the extension of arable land. Less visible but equally striking would be the breakup of Christian unity and, even more striking, the forming of nation states, with all the political, administrative, military, and ideological consequences that flowed from that development. Yet I do not think these would be the only transformations that would impress a cosmic eye surveying pre-industrial Western history. Running through these famous, world-historical developments, and accelerating, with occasional setbacks, for a thousand years, was a more elemental development, a movement of another dimension altogether and one that is more difficult to isolate and describe.

I do not know when it began—sometime in the early Middle Ages. It moved forward with varying speeds for several hundred years; was thrown back for a century or more after the first third of the fourteenth century; took a sudden lurch forward in the sixteenth century; slowed in the mid-seventeenth century; then sped precipitately ahead in the later seventeenth century to form in the eighteenth and nineteenth centuries a mighty flow that transformed at first half the globe, ultimately the whole of it, more fundamentally than any development except the Industrial Revolution. This transforming phenomenon was the movement of people outward from their original centers of habitation—the centrifugal *Völkerwanderungen* that involved an untraceable multitude of local, small-scale exoduses and colonizations, the continuous creation of new frontiers and ever-widening circumferences, the complex intermingling of peoples in the expanding border areas, and in the end the massive transfer to the Western Hemisphere of people from Africa, from the European mainland, and above all from the Anglo-Celtic offshore islands of Europe, culminating in what Bismarck called "the decisive fact in the modern world," the peopling of the North American continent.[1]

The westward transatlantic movement of people is one of the greatest events in recorded history. Its magnitudes and consequences are beyond measure. From 1500 to the present, it has involved the displacement and resettlement of over fifty million people, and it has affected indirectly the lives of uncountable millions more. It forms the foundation of American history and is basic, too, in ways we are only now beginning to understand, to the history of Europe, Africa, and even, to a lesser extent, of Asia.

This massive, global movement of people to North America and their settlement in new communities on that continent have of course attracted the attention of historians since American social history has been written. But the first, formative stage of this story—from the beginnings until the Industrial Revolution—only now, I believe, comes into sharp focus as a central historical theme: which is no criticism of the historians who have described aspects of the story as it has heretofore been seen. For scholarship proceeds dialectically; new lines of force develop to overcome deficiencies that only become visible in the wake of successful solutions to earlier deficiencies. And the outlines of such a very large subject as this come into a new configuration only at a peculiar conjunction of emerging lines of research.

Such a configuration is now taking shape, I believe, within the present creative ferment of scholarship in early American history—a wealth of research and writing concentrated on a relatively short period of time that is perhaps unique in western historiography. Books and articles on the first two centuries of European life in North America appear in a constant flow, some framed by narrowly conceived disputes with previous writers, some concluding in portentous generalities that take no account of other, similarly derived conclusions, but almost all containing new details, new information. There is an extraordinary richness in the current scholarship of this traditional field of study, and also a great confusion in understanding.[2]

The profusion and the disarray in early American history are partly the result of the sheer number of historians at work in the field. They are partly, too, the result of the fact that the subject is inevitably a battleground for general notions of the "meaning" of American life. And they are also the result of the influence of European scholarship of the same period, which has stimulated a wide array of comparative or parallel studies in American history, unintegrated into the structure of the subject as a whole. But the main reason for the disarray, I think, is simply that the sheer amount of accumulated information has overwhelmed the effective organizing principles, the major themes or interpretative structures, that have heretofore contained it. And consequently what is most urgently needed is not, at the moment, more technical studies but a fresh look at the whole story, and a general interpretation or set of related interpretations that draws together the great mass of available material—literary and statistical, new and old, local and cosmopolitan; that links latent with manifest events; and that provides a framework for a comprehensive, developmental narrative of early American history.

"The Peopling of British North America"—itself but a small segment of the saga of Western man's restless expansion across the globe—seems to contain within it the materials for one such unifying theme. The title itself is familiar, but in the context of the entire range of presently available information it takes on new meaning. It brings together the major aspects of life in the American colonies—social structure and settlement patterns, demography and politics, agriculture and religion, mobility, family organization, and ethnic relations—and places the whole evolving story of American life within the broadest possible context of Western history. "Peopling" means recruitment, emigration, and immigration, hence the whole world of overseas migration associated with the scholarship of Marcus Lee Hansen and Oscar Handlin. It implies settlement, the opening up and uses of land, mobility, and the frontier, hence the world of Frederick Jackson Turner updated by two generations of historians, most recently by the younger historical geographers, Carville Earle, R. Cole Harris, James Lemon, D. W. Meinig, H. Roy Merrens, and Robert Mitchell.[3] But it implies, too, the mingling and clashing of diverse groups and races, the evolution of social patterns, of community and family organization, population characteristics—the whole world of cultural-anthropological, social-structural, and demographic history which lies scattered in hundreds of books and articles written over the past quarter century by scholars in several disciplines pursuing separate paths of inquiry.

"Peopling" means motion, process, evolution in time, but it is not abstract: it concentrates on individuals and their fortunes. And it enlarges the perspective of early American history to the broadest possible range. For the transatlantic crossings and settlements of the colonial years were but the middle links in immense chains of related displacements and adjustments. From the jagged, wind-swept Butt of Lewis on the far northern tip of the Outer Hebrides to the Lunda kingdom deep in equatorial Africa, from Prussia south to the Danube, and from the Elbe to the Mississippi, tens of thousands of people were moving over great distances, to resettle in the alien environment of the North American seaboard communities and then to help open to initial cultivation millions of acres in the wilderness to the west. It was the greatest population movement in early modern history, and yet, despite all the recent writing on early American history, our understanding of this great westward transfer of people is a blur, lacking in structure, scale, and detail. We know only in the vaguest way who the hundreds of thousands of individuals who settled in British North America were, where precisely they came from, why they came, and how they lived out their lives. The few patches of concrete information we have bring out by contrast the vastness of our general ignorance.

The most extensive run of detailed information about any large group of immigrants in the colonial period was produced just before the Revolution by the British government, responding to fears that the mass exodus to America then under way would depopulate the realm. Such fears were exaggerated, but they were by no means ridiculous. The migration to America in the fifteen years between the end of the Seven Years War and the Revolution was remarkable by the standards of the time. Between the end of warfare in the mainland colonies and the disruption of the empire in 1775, over 55,000 Protestant Irish emigrated to America, over 40,000 Scots, and over 30,000 Englishmen—a total of approximately 125,000 from the British Isles—in addition to at least 12,000 immigrants from the German states and Switzerland who entered the port of Philadelphia, and 84,500 enslaved Africans imported to the southern mainland colonies. This grand total of about 221,500 arrivals in the fifteen-year period (a conservative figure, yet almost 10 percent of the entire estimated population of mainland America in 1775) meant an average *annual* influx of approximately 15,000 people, which was close to the total estimated population of Boston during these years; and, except for the slaves, the great majority of these tens of thousands of newcomers crowded initially into a few small port towns, almost all of them south of New England.[4]

It is therefore not at all surprising that landlords in Britain were becoming apprehensive and that pressure was exerted on the government to do something decisive to resolve the problem. By the fall of 1773, as I have elsewhere explained, it was generally believed that Parliament was considering a bill to ban all emigration to North America. The mere rumor touched off widespread debate on the legality and wisdom of such a move. Questions of national identity, of the relation of subjectship to geographical location, and of the legitimate limits of governmental power, all were discussed in newspaper columns, pamphlets, and local provincial meetings. Benjamin Franklin, then in London, wrote a carefully argued piece denouncing the contemplated legislation. And internal memoranda on the subject within the government moved the heavy inertia of the state closer to the point of action. In the end, faced with opposition and legal uncertainties, the government decided to postpone action until it knew more of the facts involved. And so, on December 9, 1773, the Treasury ordered the customs officers in England and Scotland to record the "name, age, quality, occupation, employment, and former residence" of every person leaving Great Britain for the colonies, and to register each individual's destination and reasons for leaving. The resulting data were forwarded to the Treasury, where an officer was assigned the task of scrutinizing and refining the information, and entering it in a single large workbook.

This was a pre-statistical age, and the data are faulty in many ways. In all, 9,364 permanent emigrants from Britain to the Western Hemisphere were entered on the books between December 1773 and March 1776, but com-

parison with newspaper notices of ship arrivals and studies of passenger lists reveal an underregistration of between 15 and 30 percent. And the Scottish records, though
they contain some of the most interesting information the
officials recorded, were particularly deficient in coverage.
Yet, though faulty, and though they relate only to England and Scotland, these are the most detailed transatlantic migration records we have for the eighteenth century,
and they are extremely revealing.

Results of computer analysis of these records form a
sketch of essential characteristics. A few are predictable:
the youth of these British emigrants to mainland North
America (over half were under twenty-five; over a quarter between the ages of twenty and twenty-four); the
unbalanced sex distribution (three out of four were male);
their legal status (almost half were indentured servants or
redemptioners). While almost a third traveled in family
groups, very few of the families included servants of any
kind. As to their geographical origins, just under a third
came from London and the six Home Counties of southeastern England; almost a quarter of the total came from
metropolitan London itself. On the other hand, two-fifths
of the entire group came from Scotland, and the majority
of the Scots came from the Highlands and the northern
and western islands.

These are gross figures for the recorded migration as
a whole—informative but in themselves not very surprising, and difficult to fit together into a meaningful pattern.
The more significant figures are masked by these overall
totals, and emerge only from successive stages of com-

puter analysis. In the end, the picture as a whole proves to be highly differentiated. This was no singular migration from the British Isles to North America but two separate, quite distinctive processes in motion at the same time, distinctive not only sociologically and economically but geographically as well. One consisted of emigrants who traveled outward to America from the main population center of Britain in the Thames Valley; the other group was drawn from the northern British provinces. The differences form a spectrum stretching in continuous gradations from the urban concentration of London, north across the Midlands, and into the northern counties and Scotland. At the extremities—London on the one hand, Yorkshire and the Scottish Highlands on the other —there are two distinctive patterns; the former may be designated *metropolitan*, the latter *provincial*. And these differences profoundly shaped the way these emigrants would enter into American life and the impact they would have in the new land.

The *metropolitan* pattern, which characterizes the central migration from the Thames Valley, is typified by a young man, in his early twenties, acting individually. He is not, usually, drawn from among London's most desperate, destitute slum dwellers; nor is he from the more stable or substantial segments of the population. He is, rather, an impecunious young artisan or craftsman who has served all or some part of his apprenticeship, or in a less formal way learned something of a trade, has found employment irregular or nonexistent, and, without prospects, still unmarried and without family encumbrances, has decided to head out to the colonies alone. In doing so, whether to preserve a small modicum of savings for settlement in the new land or out of sheer necessity, he has assumed a burden of debt for his transportation, to be paid off by four years of bonded labor. There are few children of either sex in this metropolitan migration, few women, and few families. The families that can be found are of the simplest possible structure—almost all of them only husband and wife or siblings traveling together.

In economic terms the typical metropolitan emigrant, though unbound by family ties or responsibilities, was not autonomous. Committed, typically, to four years of bonded servitude in the colonies, he was highly responsive to the needs of the labor market—indeed, he had no choice but to be absolutely responsive to the market in the particular corner of the colonial economy in which he found himself. Vigorous and at least in some minor way skilled in the productive work of the pre-industrial economy, these emigrants were bound to contribute to its productivity yet were prevented for four years from drawing personal gain from it, hence limited in their consumption for that period. And their natural contribution to population growth was also delayed for the period of their servitude, hence significantly diminished.

Such is the "ideal type" of the metropolitan emigrant. At the other extreme there is a different pattern altogether. In this provincial pattern the characteristic unit is not, as in the metropolitan migration, an isolated male worker in his early twenties, a bondsman for several years of unlimited servitude. It is, rather, a family, and a family that contains not only mature women but also small children, including a remarkable number of young girls. There are 7 males for every female in the metropolitan migration, but only 1.6 males for every female in the provincial. The size of these families emigrating from northern England and Scotland is surprising. The average was almost as large as the average English family in the non-emigrating population, and hence it would appear that these family units of the English population were moving essentially intact. Consistent with this fact is the economic condition of these migrating families. There are relatively few indentured servants among these provincial emigrants, even among those who were traveling alone and were in their early twenties. There would appear to have been a sufficient mobilization of resources among these families and individuals to permit freedom of movement without the severe encumbrance of bonded servitude. In one way or another—often by liquidating all their possessions, real and personal—they had raised enough, often just enough, funds to retain their freedom.

The provincial emigration was predominantly the transfer of farming families that were still in process of growth, hence likely to contribute quickly to the increase of the American population. And they would contribute quickly, too, to the growth of the American economy, not only by their constructive enterprise but by the demand they created, the markets they enlarged, as consumers. Above all, they were eager to take advantage from the start of opportunities created by the opening up of new land in America. They were likely to seek out new settlements and to move into the most attractive areas available in the backcountry. They, and not the many isolated emigrants bound in indentures to serve any master who could buy their services, were destined to be the frontiersmen in this new segment of the American population.

So much emerges clearly from the computer analysis of the customs register of emigrants of 1773–1776. But questions abound. Why did *families* leave from the northern counties and Scotland but not from the Thames Valley and the southeast generally, which in the seventeenth century had been the center of family emigrations? And why, within the northern provinces, did some families leave but not others? Is there a pattern to the immediate precipitation of decision to uproot oneself or one's family? And the questions multiply when one looks even casually at the pattern of destinations. The metropolitan migrants went mainly to a contiguous group of mid-Atlantic colonies: Pennsylvania, Maryland, and Virginia. The provincial migrants went heavily, overwhelmingly, to others: Nova Scotia, New York, and North Carolina. Why? Half of all the indentured servants and two-fifths of all the English emigrants went to the single colony of Maryland, in whose histories there is no indication that amid the political tumult of the years 1774 and 1775 approximately 2,300 immigrants (minus deaths in passage) from Britain alone (we do not know how many from elsewhere), crowded into the colony's ports and were somehow distributed along the wagon and river routes into the countryside. Why Maryland? And why was Yorkshire in particular exporting people in such numbers over such great distances? The questions arise from the computer printouts like a cloud of gnats, and one wishes one were alone, as of old, with a few literary documents that might be analyzed exhaustively, if impressionistically, down to the last syllable.

Similar questions can be asked of all of the nonslave westward-bound emigrants to North America. An estimated 10 percent of the pre-Revolutionary population was German-speaking. Why did some Germans feel impelled to leave their native villages, but not others, their immediate neighbors in apparently identical situations? About 500,000 people emigrated from southwestern Germany and Switzerland in the eighteenth century. The majority—three-fifths—went a few hundred miles north or east, to Prussia, to the Habsburg lands along the lower Danube, and, at the end of the period, at the invitation of Catherine the Great, to Russia. But two-fifths—that is, 200,000 people—from almost the identical regions, moved 4,000 miles north and then west to such exotic places as "the island," as it was commonly called in the villages of the Palatinate, of Pennsylvania.[5] Why? Were these migrations, and the similar movements of other groups—the Protestant Irish, the Dutch, and indeed the enslaved Africans—simply products of economic entrepreneurship responding rationally to developing opportunities and the need for labor? Or were there social, cultural, and economic forces behind all these movements, making them possible and determining their specific form?

And what shaped the patterns of dispersal within

America—the lines of exploration and settlement? Geography, to some extent, of course; but geography did not create the impulse to move, the dynamics of expansion; nor did sheer economic necessity or sheer demographic pressure. Nowhere in this thinly settled land did stable communities approach Malthusian limits to population growth; yet people moved continuously as if there were such pressure.[6]

The shifts of population within the colonies seem strange, irrational. In the decade preceding the Revolution, North Carolina supplied most of the first European settlers of Kentucky, but at the same time North Carolina was itself being deluged by emigrants from Pennsylvania, Virginia, Scotland, and Germany, and its population shot up from around 88,000 to somewhere between 175,000 and 185,000. Connecticut families suddenly appeared not only in northeastern Pennsylvania and the far north of the Vermont–New York border area, but also on the shores of the Gulf of Mexico. New Jerseyites settled Natchez, and were joined there by Pennsylvanians and North Carolinians. And newcomers from overseas were everywhere: Germans and Scotch-Irish could be found in almost every colony. Inland North Carolina, near present-day Fayetteville and Hillsboro, was in effect a colony of Scottish Highlanders; West Indians settled in Georgia, a colony whose population was so polyglot that a successful magistrate needed to speak fluently in at least three languages and preferably four; and Yorkshiremen and Scots arrived in increasing numbers in Nova Scotia. The road networks, once a compact tangle along the eastern seaboard, threw out new tentacles hundreds of miles across half the continent, quickly enclosing within a single communication system much of the half-billion acres east of the Mississippi.[7]

The same almost frantic expansion can be seen in every direction. For a century and a half the peopling of New England had been a gradual process, reflecting a high natural population growth without significant immigration. By the end of the seventeenth century the population had reached 90,000 to 100,000. For half a century thereafter new towns had been settled at an average rate of six a year; by 1760 the vacant central area had been filled and the population had reached an estimated 500,000. In the next decade and a half, while the population rose another 20 percent, no fewer than 264 new towns were settled, an average of 18 a year. Who settled these remote towns? Where did the settlers come from, and why? We know something about Benning Wentworth's entrepreneurship in creating these townships and we know something of the efforts that were made to recruit settlers for them from overseas. But we know nothing of how Wentworth and his associates in New Hampshire assembled the several thousand proprietors' names, or what the relationships between the settlers and the proprietors were, or what conditions had set in motion this remarkable domestic migration into these isolated northern villages.[8]

There are occasional patches of light—a few faces, a few statistics here and there in the current literature to illuminate the peopling of America over the first century and a half of European settlement. There are some excellent regional studies that bear on migration, written mainly by historical geographers[9]; a comprehensive and illuminating study of over seven hundred participants in the great Puritan migration[10]; an economic analysis of the recruitment characteristics of indentured servants, which complements an older, less statistical study[11]; two highly suggestive probes by Mildred Campbell—bold, innovative, seminal studies which, twenty years after their appearance, have become the focuses of interpretative controversies[12]; a few imaginative studies of slavery and the recruitment of slaves[13]; and a number of reliable community studies, some of the most interesting of which relate not to New England, the subject of the first of such efforts, but to Virginia and especially to Maryland, the work of the excellent group of historians associated with the St. Mary's City Commission.[14]

Still, despite all of these writings, and, in addition, my own effort to describe comprehensively the emigration from Britain on the eve of the Revolution, the population movements of the pre-industrial era, multitudinous and complex almost beyond description, remain mysterious and chaotic. There are no structural lines, no general propositions, to frame the history as a whole—nor will there be until the dimensions of the subject are recognized for what they are and the possibility of a unified organization for the story as a whole clearly seen.

It is in order to suggest something, at least, of these dimensions in concrete terms, and to sketch a few of the general elements in the overall story, that I would like to put forward four propositions, or broad lines of interpretation. They are tentative, and they are admittedly limited in coverage. They do not involve to any significant extent the movements of either of the two non-Caucasian peoples—the Native Americans and the Africans—whose histories are so vital a part of the story. For, despite the mass of writing, much of it polemical, that is available on both of these groups, we know as yet relatively little about their histories; we have nothing like the density of information about them that is available for other groups.[15]

The propositions that follow are therefore only a limited starting point in approaching a very large subject. They are meant simply to illustrate the dimensions of the subject and the possibility of controlling it within certain discrete lines of interpretation.

Proposition One

The peopling of British North America was an extension outward and an expansion in scale of domestic mobility in the lands of the immigrants' origins, and the transatlantic flow must be understood within the context of these <u>domestic</u> mobility patterns. Ultimately, however, its development introduced a new and dynamic force in European population history, which permanently altered the traditional configuration.

If there is one uncontroversial fact that has emerged from the past three decades of research in European social history, it is that the traditional society of early modern Europe was a mobile society—a world in motion. Professor E. E. Rich, in a perceptive article on the population of Elizabethan England written thirty-six years ago, stressed the relationship between domestic migration and overseas migration. Rich found a persistence rate in selected Elizabethan villages over a ten-year period of no more than 50 percent. He estimated that only 16 percent of all Elizabethan families had remained in the same village as long as a century.[16] Since Rich wrote, the picture has been greatly elaborated—by local historians like Alan Everitt, by historical geographers like John H. C. Patten, and by members of the Cambridge Group for the History of Population and Social Structure.[17]

We now know not simply that the English population was mobile in the pre-industrial era but that its mobility was a composite of three closely interwoven patterns. First, there was a pattern of short-distance movements found everywhere in the English countryside, resulting from population growth; decline in real wages; the extension of commercial farming, which demanded, and helped create, an army of rural wage laborers; and the uprooting effect of domestic industry. Everywhere unattached farmworkers roamed the countryside seeking employment. Among more established groups, too, short-distance mobility in the countryside was common, in part the result of the circulation of the young among households of higher or equal status, compounded by the ubiquity of servitude. Roger Schofield has estimated that, in the typical English village of the eighteenth century, three out of every four males between the ages of fifteen and nineteen had left home and were in service of some kind; typically, two out of every three children of both sexes left their home parishes, to be replaced by children of other parishes. Overall, at any given time in the seventeenth century, 14 percent of the total population was in service, and around one-half of all the people in England were, or had been, servants. This generality of servitude meant widespread movement—yet movements that did not totally disconnect individuals from their original environments. Most of those who left home young to labor in other households or enterprises remained within half a day's walking distance of their homes.[18]

The second pattern was regional: mobility over longer distances, funneling a significant portion of the mobile population of the countryside into provincial towns and cities. Thus the historical geographer John H. C. Patten, in his study of mobility in seventeenth-century East Anglia—the original source of much of the New England population—demonstrates that the constant flow of country people into the three urban centers of Norwich, Great Yarmouth, and Ipswich had its sources in communities within a range of eight to twenty miles of those towns. He suggests that the larger the urban magnet the wider the geographical range of recruitment and the deeper the poverty of the migrants, especially among those beyond the usual early years of high mobility. A further specification is offered by Peter Clark, examining the flow of people into and out of three Kentish towns at the time of the first British American settlements. He too finds a direct correlation between size of towns and the distances traveled by immigrants into them, the main recruitment range for these Kentish towns being a radius of sixteen miles; but he goes beyond that to establish a further correlation between socio-economic level and distance of recruitment.

He distinguishes between, on the one hand, the "betterment migration" of the quite young sons of stable rural families moving short distances into towns, usually for apprenticeship training; and, on the other hand, the "subsistence migration" of groups of much poorer people forced to move over greater distances simply to survive —to move more frequently, and to move more commonly from town to town rather than from country to town. These are true wanderers, isolated individuals far from their original residences, dislodged originally by poverty or the fear of poverty, roaming the land alone or in small groups, seeking employment and security, picking up casual labor whenever possible and repelled back, after temporary employment, into the migrating stream of poor people wandering through the countryside.

But the high correlation between distance and poverty was significantly reduced in the passage of time. By the early eighteenth century these long-distance subsistence migrants—common in the sixteenth and early seventeenth centuries—had largely disappeared as population had grown, agriculture had expanded, the mortality crises in the towns had diminished, the demand for manufactured goods had increased, and vagrancy legislation had become more stringent. By the mid-eighteenth century "long distance migration [was] . . . no longer closely identified with the lower orders. Instead, upper social groups—gentlemen and merchants, as well as professional men—registered the greatest average distances travelled." But all of these regional migrations, whatever their socio-economic character and their spatial dimensions, tended to remove people from their immediate home environments, despite the efforts that were made to preserve connections of some sort, especially within extended kin networks.

The third and by far the most dynamic pattern was superimposed over all the local and regional movements. This "dominant node in the national migration system" was the great flow of people into the vast and constantly growing catch basin of London. London grew enormously in this era: reasonable population estimates are 60,000 in the early sixteenth century, 200,000 in 1600, 350,000 in 1650, and 575,000 in 1700, at which time greater London contained 11 percent of the entire population of England and Wales. And this growth was no product of natural population surpluses in the city itself. London devoured people. Disease devastated the slums; yet ever more people flocked in from all over the realm to restore the losses. Plague deaths of some 15 percent of the total were made up, in the seventeenth century, within two years.[19]

One can only guess at the overall numbers of those who left the countryside or small towns for London. Patten estimates that one million migrants came to London between 1550 and 1750. E. A. Wrigley calculates that in the period 1650–1750 deaths so far exceeded births in London that only a *net* immigration into the city of eight thousand persons a year can account for London's

growth, and therefore that London was absorbing approximately one-half of the entire natural increase in England's population. One in every six English adults in this
period had a direct experience of life in London, and
one-third of London's population at any point in the
century were recent arrivals. The movement to London
flowed predominantly from northwest to southeast across
Scotland and England, and as it flowed it drew off elements of the lesser mobility patterns by means of subnet-
works connecting it to the migrations to provincial cities
like Norwich, Sheffield, and York.[20]

All of this may seem remote from the settling of the
farms and villages of colonial America, but in fact it is
essential to understanding it. For, in its earliest phase, the
peopling of North America was a spillover—an out-
growth, an extension—of these established patterns of
mobility in England. It tapped into these existing flows
without basically altering them or modifying their magnitudes.

Thus, while it is of course true that religion shaped the
leadership, organization, and ethos of the Puritan migration of the early seventeenth century, the human con-
stituents were available in the East Anglian population
accustomed for generations to move geographically in
search of employment, opportunity, and stability. In the
context of the mobility of the time, the famous Puritan
exodus—which, to judge by the weight of subsequent
scholarship, must have been a world-historical event—as
an organized migration was nothing remarkable. The traditional figure (which is probably high) is 21,200 emi-

grants to Puritan New England in the twelve years before 1642; but during those same years three times that number left England for other colonies in America and the West Indies, and almost six times that number of Englishmen and Scots (120,000) migrated to Ireland. In one 24-*month* period in the 1630s, at least 10,000 Scots migrated to Ireland, roughly half the total of the entire Puritan migration.[21]

Amid this continuous circulation of people throughout the greater British world, the relocation of religious groups like the Puritans, seeking relief and self-determination, was by no means "unique in the annals of migration."[22] Such events were in fact commonplace in this highly mobile society. Most Puritan emigrants, one English historian has written, were normal Englishmen acting normally. Unemployed west-country laborers flocked into Bristol just as East Anglians did into Norwich, and since Bristol had long been the departure point for western voyages it was natural for them to extend their search for employment to the shores of Virginia and Maryland. The Atlantic became a highway like the Great North Road, and it was a highway rather easier to cross, despite all the dangers of ocean voyages, than the land passages across the British Isles. People learned to move west naturally, just as they moved north, south, and east, seeking employment, security, and a hopeful future.[23]

We do not yet have a detailed explanation of precisely how, in these early years, the transition from domestic to overseas migration—the bulging out in an unaccustomed direction—took place in England. We do know how it happened elsewhere. Just such a transition from domestic mobility to overseas migration has been described in the case of Spain. We know how it was that impoverished Andalusian farmworkers and the idle *hidalgos* and tradesmen of the overcrowded southern cities moved off to Spain's American colonies.[24] And students of French population movements have explained the nature of such transitions in mobility patterns, and particularly the shift from temporary movements to permanent migrations.[25] Yet, though the connections between domestic mobility and overseas migration have not been explained in detail in the English case, there are some revealing clues in the available material.

When poverty in the countryside led to severe population pressure in the towns, indigent migrants were dealt with harshly—expelled from town to town, thrown into houses of correction, isolated in disreputable slums, banished to riotous suburbs. The farther away the better: some town authorities managed by one means or another to ship some of these "subsistence migrants," already used to long-distance migration, to America.[26] More important, the normal workings of the labor market, by a natural extension, somehow reached overseas. For it appears that the incidence of emigration in the seventeenth century relates positively to harvest failures in England and negatively to rises in wage levels. And there seems to be some degree of correlation between the movements of seventeenth-century Chesapeake tobacco prices and the flows of indentured servants—a correlation that can be explained only by the presence of a ready pool of available recruits and well-established mechanisms for translating the demands of the labor market into the movements of large numbers of people. Such mechanisms operated in the domestic labor markets: the ebb and flow of seasonal labor migrations depended upon them; somehow they were extended to the developing labor markets overseas, with the result that the Chesapeake tobacco fields in the seventeenth century became an annex to the labor markets of southwestern England.[27]

Though the precise workings of the links between the domestic and overseas labor markets remain somewhat vague, the fact seems undeniable that migration to British North America in its first phases was a bulging out, an extension, of domestic mobility patterns into overseas territories, with results of the greatest importance. We now know, for example, that it was the failure of the southern English labor supply to provide the manpower needed in the expanding Chesapeake tobacco fields that led to the first large-scale importation of black slaves. All the correlations are consistent: the rising numbers of indentured servants through the 1650s, then the falling away in the sixties, as English population growth slackened, as fire and plague both reduced the available labor supply in London and created a greater demand there, and hence as real wages rose. All of this tended to consume what labor there was in domestic markets, while the imports of slaves in Virginia and Maryland rose significantly. Blacks did not outnumber whites in the labor force of the tobacco colonies until the 1680s, and thereafter, as the scale of production continued to rise, the dependence on an

almost endless supply of black laborers became permanent.[28]

Again and again major issues, apparently unresolvable
paradoxes in the peopling process, can be resolved by
reference to the *domestic* scene in the land of origin. The
situation in the Scottish Highlands in the mid- to late
eighteenth century appears at first bewildering. Emigration was said to be a universal phenomenon, an epidemic,
a madness that gripped the minds of ordinary people,
celebrated in song and poetry, denounced in endless
newspaper columns and official statements, and the object
of desperate concern by landlords and officials. But were
the thousands who were leaving rich or poor, transient or
permanent, burdens or benefits to the community, hence
losses or gains in their exodus for the country at large? On
the one hand, the explanations offered at the time stressed
the dreadful poverty of those who left, the desperation of
their living conditions, and the devastation they had faced
from the new rent rises and other economic changes. On
the other hand, there were constant complaints that the
emigrants were draining off thousands of pounds a year
in loose capital. And indeed a single shipload, about
which we happen to know a great deal, leaving from the
barren, austere north-Scottish county of Caithness, almost devoid of surplus capital, drained off approximately
£1,000 in cash or its equivalent. Paradox—but it is resolved if one views the whole of the Highlands emigration, domestic and overseas, comprehensively.

The Highlanders, their lives badly dislocated by the
destruction of the clan system after the suppression of the

Jacobite rebellion of 1745 and dislocated too by the in-creasing rationalization of agricultural production, were moving away in droves—but not all to the same areas. The overseas migration was managed largely by tacks-men (primary lessees) or shipping entrepreneurs, who organized expeditions of freight-paying passengers, and a shipload of such emigrants was obliged to pay up to £800 collectively for their passage. Many, in addition, took an "overplus" of funds with them for accidents and extras along the way. To manage this, often they sold all their possessions: but they were not the abject poor. Yet the truly impoverished left too—not commonly, however, for America. Instead, they moved off to the Lowlands, where they helped to provide the labor force needed in the growing industries and the service markets of the cities. The distinction was explained, in 1805, by Francis Horner, who knew the facts. With the breakup of the clan system and the commercialization of agriculture, he wrote in an essay on Lord Selkirk's *Observations . . . on Emigration* (Edinburgh, 1805), a large part of the working population, especially in the Highlands, was displaced and rendered economically redundant.

Two prospects present themselves. In the Low Country of Scotland, the wages of manufacturing labour; in America, the easy acquisition of land in absolute property . . . but the execution of the latter plan must be attended with more expense than the other. It will be practicable, therefore, to those only who can afford this expense. . . . The cotters have seldom property enough for the necessary expenses of emigration; and few of them have ever been able to emigrate: they have, in general, removed into the manufacturing districts of the Low Country of Scotland. But the population of the Highlands was composed, in a very large proportion, of the small tenants; and all of these are possessed of something that might be denominated capital. Most of them live much more wretchedly, as to habitation and diet, than the labourers who earn daily wages in other parts of the island; but they have property of greater value. . . . By disposing of all this stock, especially if the price of cattle happens to be high, [the small tenant] is enabled to embark in undertakings which cannot be thought of by the cotter, and which are not within the reach of the peasantry, even in the more improved and richer parts of the island.

To those who can thus afford the expenses of the passage and first settlement, the low price of land in America presents the prospect of speedily attaining a situation and mode of life similar to that in which all their habits have been formed. . . . By their ability or inability to afford the expenses of their passage to America, the choice of the Highlanders, with a very few exceptions, has been entirely regulated. Even among those whose poverty forced them to go at first into the manufacturing towns, some of the most remarkable exertions of industry have been prompted, only by the desire of accumulating as much money as might enable them to join their friends beyond the Atlantic.[29]

So when the tacksmen on the MacLeod estates on the island of Harris in the Outer Hebrides, prosperous before the MacLeods elevated the rents, contemplated drastic action, they refused to consider buying property in the Lowlands. Like so many Highlanders, they had been affected by that "spirit of emigration," a contemporary reported, "which in a few years will carry the inhabitants of the Highlands and Islands of Scotland into North America. Disdaining to become possessors of farms in the low countries [of Scotland] and follow the customs of its inhabitants which they held in contempt, they launched out into a new world breathing a spirit of liberty and a desire of every individual becoming a proprietor, where they imagine they can still obtain land for themselves and their flocks of cattle at a triffling rent or of conquering it from the Indians with the sword."[30] The migration to North America, in this case as in others, was not an isolated phenomenon but one element in a larger configuration, the whole of which explains the differences among the parts.

Similar dispersals took place in other areas that contributed significantly to the peopling of British North America—Ireland and the German states particularly; in these cases too emigration was at first a spillover of domestic population movements.

Mobility was endemic in southwestern Germany, throughout the Rhine Valley, in parts of Switzerland, and in the Low Countries. Many of the most "traditional" German villages had long been the scenes of high mobility. Through the whole broad band of central Europe there was a constant short-distance flow of village workers seeking seasonal employment and permanent improvement; here too, as in Britain, regional urban centers drained off the mobile population of the local hinterlands; and here too religion gave shape to small portions of the

general mobility—all of this quite without reference to
the special problems created by persecution, wars, and
famine in the Palatinate at the end of the seventeenth
century. Sects in central Europe, stimulated in their mobility by the political and religious fragmentation of the
German-speaking world, drew aside in self-protection
just as the Pilgrims and Puritans had done; many sought
resolutions of their problems in more extensive movements than they had originally intended.[31]

A thousand local rivulets fed streams of emigrants
moving through northern and central Europe in all directions—*east* more commonly than west. A sampling of the
sources of the first sizable German migration to British
territory, which scattered ultimately to Ireland and New
York—that of 1709–1710—shows a remarkable range of
communities from which the migrants came. Approximately 42 percent of the immigrants came from the Palatinate proper, west of the Rhine and south of the Mosel.
But as many came from east of the Rhine, and there were
groups from the farthest borderlands of the German-
speaking world—from as far north as Flensburg, the Bal-
tic port a few miles from Denmark; from as far east as the
Czech border towns of Dresden and Görlitz; and from as
far west and south as Montbéliard, an Alsatian Huguenot
community in the suzerainty of Württemberg, close to
Basel and Besançon.[32] This was no concentrated exodus
with a singular impetus, but a kind of seepage from an
otherwise almost invisible but continuous and normal
flow of people from village to village, from village to
town, and from town to city. The Palatinate, it has been

suggested—long before America was thought of in such terms—was a melting pot of European peoples.[33]

At times, in the general swirl, the very identity of the migrants got lost, compounding the difficulty of identifying particular motives and distinctions. The so-called "Palatines" were by no means all from the two Palatinates: anyone voyaging down the Rhine was likely to acquire that name—Swiss as well as Westphalians, Alsatians and Bavarians as well as Hessians.[34] Similarly, some of the so-called "Germans" who settled in Pennsylvania were not "Pennsylvania Dutch" (that is, *Deutsch* = German) at all, but, paradoxically, *really* Dutch—that is, Netherlanders, Dutch-speaking migrants from the border region of the Netherlands, who had moved first to German territory before going overseas as "Germans."[35] The same kind of jumble took place in the eastward migrations; emigrants to Hungary and then to Russia from Württemberg, Baden, Hesse, the Palatinate, and even Alsace were lumped together as "Swabians" or "Saxons."[36] And when a group of French Protestants, having left France for the Rhineland, ended up, after a second migration, on the banks of the Kennebec River in Maine, their sponsors chose to refer to them as "Germans," though they could not have been more French, and apparently succeeded in passing them off as Germans—happily, since it helped remove New Englanders' suspicions that they might be clandestine Catholics or secretly sympathetic to New France.[37]

All of this is particularly well documented. For, in the mosaic of small princedoms and dukedoms that made up

Germany, the continuing allegiance of taxpaying subjects and agricultural workers was considered to be essential, and consequently movement was scrutinized and recorded. Departures were legalized by the issuance of formal documents, most often letters of manumission, many hundreds of which have survived. Through them one can trace the departures and destinations of large numbers of people who were in motion in these German principalities, establish their economic and social status by noting the taxes they were obliged to pay upon their departures, and perhaps find clues to their motivations and expectations. And the manumission records contain only the most obvious of the many traces that remain of this widely dispersed emigration. Church records and court files on both sides of the Atlantic extend the documentation, as do shipping lists, arrival records, and correspondence sent back from America to relatives, friends, and officials in a hundred German villages and towns.[38]

At times the seepage that made up the early German migrations can be studied almost microscopically. One finds, for example, in the records of the obscure hamlet of Heuchelheim in the northeastern corner of the Palatinate, official notice of the legal emigration of seventy-four adults and at least fourteen children in the twenty-two years after 1749. Most of the adults declared their intention of marrying and settling in villages of the Palatinate or in the neighboring Archbishopric of Worms; but there were a few exceptions. One man left to join the Prussian army; one family with numerous children went four miles off to the town of Frankenthal to work in a porcelain factory; and three unattached men and two complete families departed—we do not know why—for Pennsylvania, four thousand miles away. Of these future American families—about to confront over forty toll barriers on the Rhine, profiteering shippers and Dutch authorities in Rotterdam, British officials in Cowes or Portsmouth, and then an ocean voyage of many weeks—one was declared to be so poor it could not be charged the usual tax. All four members, therefore, would be sold into servitude if the cost of their passage was not "redeemed" upon their arrival in Philadelphia.[39]

The same natural spillover of domestic population movements, whatever the determination of direction, is found everywhere. The first movements to America from Scotland and Ireland, whenever they occurred, were not different from those from England, from the German states, from Switzerland, or from the Low Countries. In the early phases of the migrations the existing *patterns* of mobility in these homelands were unaffected by the American magnet, the demographic *structure* remained constant. The North American colonies were simply another destination available to people in motion.

But in time the dynamics of the situation changed. Everywhere, though in different phasings, the pull of the American colonies grew to the point where it shaped the patterns of European domestic mobility. It became an independent force acting on the demographic configurations of the Old World, a powerful and ungovernable prod outside all indigenous propulsions, created by entrepreneurship, promotion, and the sheer magnetism of economic betterment and religious toleration.

The slave trade was only the extreme expression of the deliberate engineering of overseas migration. William Penn's famous efforts at promoting emigration and settlement, like the earlier efforts of the Virginia Company and of the other early proprietors, were relatively passive: in effect Penn ran an advertising campaign sufficient to mobilize elements of a readily available population.[40] But in time truly dynamic entrepreneurs of migration appeared, and the flows of emigration to North America were propelled forward by them. Agents for shippers and land companies combed the Rhineland and the British Isles for emigrants, and lent support to emigration organizations formed by would-be migrants themselves. At this stage there was no spontaneous, mechanical relationship between poverty and emigration. The only correlation that can be firmly established is between the activities of recruiting agents and the flow of emigrants from areas with a high degree of actual or latent mobility, especially areas from which people had already emigrated to America. And the recruiters could succeed because the maturing American economy, while superficially providing less of an open opportunity than it had earlier, was basically more expansive, more elaborate, more attractive than it had been before, and its magnetism persisted, at times grew.

Parcels of prime coastal land obtainable in freehold tenure were obviously less easily available in the eighteenth century than they had been in the early and mid-

seventeenth century; in many areas such land was completely unobtainable. But there were millions of open
acres east of the Mississippi, and the growing scale of
enterprise, both in commerce and agriculture, and the
multiplying and maturing towns created opportunities
that had not existed when coastal property had been almost free for the taking. In the mid-eighteenth century
the opportunities available in the American world were
opening up, not closing down, though they were taking
different form. This fact radiated out into susceptible
populations in great sweeps of enticing information
propagated by paid recruiters, and the impact on the
established mobility patterns in Europe was profound.[41]

So in Paisley, Scotland, in 1773, when weavers struck
for higher wages and blocked employers' efforts to use
scab labor, the authorities undertook a resolute, all-out
prosecution of the ringleaders for creating "an unlawful
combination"—until they discovered that several thousand of the workers "threatened to go off in a body to
America." At that point the trial became, in the words of
one of the judges, "very delicate." The court drew back
and imposed lenient sentences, and not on all but only on
some of the leaders, freeing the rest; the judges contented
themselves with lecturing all concerned on "the criminal-
ity of their conduct." Privately, the chief judge breathed
a sigh of relief that "all thoughts of going over to America
are for the present laid aside."[42]

The presence of the powerful American magnet had
become a wild card, an autonomous force in the demographic situation. The question is not why the British

government undertook a comprehensive study of the causes and consequences of emigration to America in 1773 but why it had not done so before. For, while the fact that the mainland North American colonies were British led to the natural assumption that movement from Britain to America should be as free as from England to Scotland or Ireland, it took no great insight to see that the effect of continuing mass emigration might prove to be extremely complicated for Britain. And indeed, by 1767 there was concern enough about the consequences of "so great a number of useful inhabitants . . . daily emigrating to the American colonies" for the British government to disallow an act of the Georgia legislature subsidizing the immigration and resettlement of British subjects in newly opened territories, a common practice that had been engaged in by South Carolina since 1731. But there were no general guidelines for regulating mobility within British territory, and landlords like the powerful Anglo-Irish secretary of state for the colonies, Lord Hillsborough, contemplating the possible depopulation of their estates, were beginning to demand them. It was an awkward and difficult problem which few in authority in Britain fully understood.[43]

For other nations, which could not imagine profiting even indirectly from the exodus to America except by the elimination of criminals and indigents, there were no such complications. Officials in the German states had long been aware of the danger posed by what one of them called "the frivolous itch of emigration" to such outlandish places as *"Bintzel Vannier,"* as Pennsyl-vania was

called in the Main River Valley. They tried to control the
flow. They levied stiff *Steuer* (taxes) on the emigrants,
followed by stiffer *Nachsteuer;* tied up manumissions and
exits in all sorts of red tape; and frequently prohibited
emigration altogether.[44] But given the weakness of state
power in the eighteenth century, the exodus could not be
stopped. It continued forcefully until the outbreak of the
Revolutionary War.

Thus Wrigley's assertion that London in the years
1650–1750 was absorbing one-half of the entire natural
increase of population in the English countryside reflects
one of the basic facts of eighteenth-century social life in
Britain. But in the period 1640–1699, Wrigley has more
recently shown, 69 percent of all of England's natural
increase was drawn off not by London but by emigration
to North America, and over the whole period from 1695
to 1801 emigration consumed 20 percent of the natural
increase of England.[45] Hence there was in effect not *one*
"dominant node in the national migration system"; there
were *two*. The whole configuration of British mobility
was fundamentally affected by the exodus to America.
London was the most common source of American immigrants—it had been that at the beginning and it remained
that throughout the colonial period. Much of the movement to London, it now appears, was only a stage in the
migration to America. And indeed I wonder, if we had
all the information we needed—if we could establish the
magnitude and phasing of transatlantic migration from all
parts of Britain, and if we could establish the precise
relation of overseas migration to other aspects of popula-

tion movements—I wonder if we would not conclude that the peopling of North America became a dominant force in the history of British mobility in the later years of colonial rule, a powerful determinant of its shape.

The key element in this complex picture is the linkage between local migrations and overseas emigration, and that association, as I say, is extraordinarily difficult to isolate and describe. But a certain eighteenth-century Shetlander, John Harrower, whose career is particularly well documented, would, I think, have understood it precisely. His experiences exemplify at least one aspect of this process vividly, and he was a reflective man.

One of the ten thousand emigrants registered by the customs officials, he recorded his experiences and feelings in a detailed and expressive diary. He was an impoverished forty-year-old shopkeeper and tradesman who in December 1773 left his home in Lerwick in the far Shetland Islands, north of the Scottish mainland, "in search of business," carrying with him his total capital of 8 ½ pence cash and £3 worth of woolen stockings for sale along the way. He never intended to go to America: his aim was to find employment in Britain or the Low Countries, restore his finances, and then return home. After repeated failures to find work in Scotland or to obtain a passage across the North Sea, he took a free berth to Portsmouth and then, hopeful of employment in the capital, walked the eighty miles to London. There he found a mass of similarly unemployed and desperate artisans and tradesmen, some of them reduced to beggary. He held out as long as he could, but having spent his last shilling without finding work, alone "in a garret room . . . frendless and forsaken," he sold himself for four years of bonded servitude to a shipmaster going to Virginia in return for the cost of his voyage.

On board the *Planter* he found seventy-four other indentured servants drawn from all over the British Isles but recruited also from among the lesser artisans of London. A wide range of trades was represented—a glassblower from Surrey, a wigmaker from Southwark, a watchmaker from London, a breeches-maker from Wiltshire, a butcher from Ireland, a footman, a groom, a boatmaker, a painter—but no one without a stated occupation, no simple laborer or farmworker below the status of a husbandman. After a voyage lasting two months, the ship docked at the town of Fredericksburg, Virginia, on the Rappahannock River, where the shipmaster disposed of his human cargo. Most of the servants on board were bought by a merchant jobber, who resold them individually and with careful calculation of the interests of potential buyers. Harrower's years of service were bought by Colonel William Daingerfield, who needed a tutor for his children, and the Scotsman ended up on the Daingerfield plantation, Belvidera, where he found security and even a measure of gentility, though not the independence he sought. He was still in service there, a schoolteacher and respected domestic servant, when he died in 1777, possessed of £70 with which he was planning to bring over his wife and three children.[46]

So in complex ways the American magnet exerted its force. For some, it was a distant but positive goal somehow to be reached; for others, it was a last resort, a refuge when all else failed; for still others, it was a mystery full of vague possibilities, to be explored, considered, realized, or rejected. But for everyone in this mobile world it was an irreducible fact of life, ever present and ever potent.

11

The Rings of Saturn

I began the first lecture with reference to an imaginary satellite. I want to begin this one with reference to the astonishing interstellar journey of the Voyager spacecraft. By November 1980 Voyager I, that fabulous little machine crammed with detecting gadgets, had traveled a billion miles from home and had come within thirty thousand miles of the rings of Saturn, the beautiful flat disk that has evoked such romantic responses since people first detected it in studying the heavens. Voyager I, and then Voyager II soon after it, brought the human eye up close, and the mysteries, the wonder, and some of the beauty were dispelled. We now know what the rings actually are—trillions of ice particles, some the size of microscopic dust, some the size of automobiles, some larger than cathedrals—hurtling endlessly in great heaps and showers around the planet in regular courses shaped by gravitational force. Everything seems strange up that close. The Cassini division, believed to be empty space between two rings, proves to contain a whole system of ringlets invisible from earth. Mysterious spokes of

light shoot vertically across the plane of the rings. Unknown moons appear—in all, sixteen have been discovered, and there are undoubtedly more—some of which
orbit together and slip around each other in a braidlike
fashion.

So in the end, as the data come in and are registered,
what appeared at a distance to be a beautifully clear and
distinct plane of rings around the planet proves to be
reflections of light on torrential multitudes of ice blocks
and dust, whose characteristics and the patterns of whose
movements scientists must now begin to examine as they
have not done before.

Historical discovery, it seems to me, develops similarly. At first we view things from afar, and find clear and
gross configurations. Then we learn more, and then
more; and at special times, by special developments—the
discovery of unknown personal documents, statistical
compilations, new and imaginative uses of familiar documents, computers—we suddenly come up close, like
Voyagers I and II, and see a world in detail that is very
different from what we imagined from afar. Puritanism,
for example. Puritanism, we now know, was no unified
historical phenomenon, even in its New England form.
Up close, it proves to be a range of beliefs, ideas, and
attitudes, clustering into shifting and unstable groupings.
If there ever was an "orthodoxy" in colonial New England it was nothing stable and nothing intrinsic to the
religion itself but a socio-ecclesiastical program whose
promoters gained a precarious ascendancy within a society boiling with "dissident" beliefs and sects. The "dissi-
dents," the "radicals," in seventeenth-century New En-

gland—separatists, Anabaptists, Quakers, extreme millenarians, spiritists, antinomians, Socinians, Gortonists, and miscellaneous seekers—were no less "Puritan" than the elder Winthrop and his clerical establishment. They were only less well organized, less stable, and less successful, and hence have been less carefully observed by historians; only recently have they been restored to their proper place in the historical galaxy.[1] Similarly, the colonial merchant class. Assumed to be a singular, distinctive historical entity, it was once the subject of much historical discussion and was assigned a special role in the advent of the Revolution. But seen up close, it dissolves into a spectrum of social and entrepreneurial types whose one common characteristic, wholesale trading, in no way united them as a meaningful group, political or social.[2]

So it is with population history. We once knew, or thought we knew, who the people of British North America were, how they arrived, how they settled, and the character of the society and culture they helped create here. But up close—through intensive studies of origins and recruitment, of the process of settlement, of community organization, of everyday culture, and of growth rates and family structure—they look quite different from what we had imagined.

My second proposition, therefore, is the following:

Proposition Two

Examination of the settlement and development patterns for the whole of British North America reveals not uniformity, but highly differentiated processes, which form the context of the immigrants' arrival. The fortunes of the arriving newcomers must be seen against this varied and shifting background.

"New England towns" have been thought of as constituting a distinctive category of human association. From Herbert Baxter Adams in the 1880s to Michael Zuckerman and Edward Cook almost a century later, historians have sought to depict the common characteristics of these clusterings, assuming any particular town to be in some way a variation of a basic ideal form. And of course the New England towns in the seventeenth and eighteenth centuries did have certain common characteristics. But as population centers these communities differed significantly. In their founding they had been only a collection of what have been called "loosely joined fragments" of a common culture and society, with variant appearances, land usages, religious practices, military organizations, and politics. In economic terms there were at least three distinct zones in the seventeenth century:

an urbanized coastal region . . . a subsistence farming region . . . and an area of highly commercialized agriculture, such as the towns of the colony's breadbasket—the Connecticut River Valley. Each region had different patterns of social relations, economic opportunity, and political behavior. Throughout the seventeenth century, the levels of communal harmony, social stratification, and political elitism displayed a wide diversity in each of the three zones . . . each zone had a distinct "ensemble of social relations."[3]

It is the variations in their demographic roles, however, that are most relevant in the peopling process. At any stage, some of the towns were absorbing people, others were propelling them outward, and there was no regular, short-distance seasonal pulsation of migration as there was in the British countryside. If the movements of people among these villages had left traces on a photographic plate they would show up, first, as a multitude of short lines forming together a penumbra around each town and joining it with neighboring towns (lines representing marriage associations and the movements of sons of certain families to newly opened nearby land); and second, as irregular streaks of some length, moving out of *certain* towns, not all, at *certain* stages of their development, and going in *certain* directions, not all. At any particular time some towns were dynamic centers of small galaxies; others were recipient satellites; still others were almost entirely autonomous worlds—isolated but evolving little colonies within a colony, scarcely part of the greater firmament at all. Everywhere the scene was shifting constantly, as towns grew, families proliferated, people moved, fresh land and new towns were opened and settled, and new patterns of migration took shape and then dissolved. The population history of the region as a whole was extremely complex, and it is not easily susceptible to measurement or comprehensive description.[4]

James Henretta, in an interesting essay, attempted to define a distinctive growth pattern for the evolution of these communities in the light of the demographic data contained in the first statistical community studies of colonial New England. He hypothesized a developmental cycle of three distinctive periods in the social life of these towns, corresponding to the passage of three generations: a phase of traditional community life, a phase of high expansion and growth, and a static phase, largely in the late eighteenth century.[5] But, as Darrett Rutman subsequently made clear in a critical study of this pattern as it relates to the New Hampshire towns of the eighteenth century, this formula is too simple a description.[6] Something more complex is needed—perhaps a spiral pattern rather than a cycle: that is, towns going through similar evolutions but at significantly different stages of a general, overall regional development. However that may be, any single formulation that succeeds in capturing the variety of community life, even in so seemingly uniform a region as New England, will have to be exceedingly subtle.

As with the New England towns, so with other population centers—Pennsylvania's towns, for example, whose pre-industrial street patterns, indicators of differing culture areas, have been classified into four major categories, with various subgroupings[7]; and above all the cities of colonial America. Nothing has inhibited thought on urban development more than the assumption that a city is a city is a city—that all cities, because that is their nature, have similar characteristics (they all have to have sewers, a water supply, police, poorhouses, social stratification, churches, etc.), and the duty of the historian is to show how they acquired these necessary, hence historically inevitable, characteristics. But in demographic terms the colonial urban centers varied greatly. They had distinctive origins, growth patterns, and functions, and they had different roles in society at large. What, in precise terms, these origins and economic and social functions were is still very much a matter of discussion. But it is certain that these communities differed, and while all urban agglomerations have some common features, the distinctions among them, more than their similarities, shaped the ways in which new arrivals were absorbed into the society.[8]

Thus, as noted before, London in the eighteenth century was a graveyard; it devoured multitudes not only of its natives but of the surplus population of the country-side migrating into the metropolis year after year and decade after decade. And the provincial English cities were similarly absorptive and destructive throughout this period, though on a smaller scale. But, though epidemics swept the colonial cities too and though the death rates there too were high, these American urban communities were not graveyards in the same sense: they had quite different roles in population history, which may be suggested by different metaphors. If London and the provincial English cities were graveyards, Boston was a nursery, Philadelphia was a human warehouse, and New York was a staging center for the distribution of immigrants into the far northern frontier.

Of Boston's pre-Revolutionary population history we are surprisingly ignorant. Almost every estimate of its numbers goes back to a single undocumented statement by Lemuel Shattuck in 1846. According to that estimate the population rose slowly to approximately sixteen thousand around 1740, and then leveled off there until the Revolution. Assuming that that is at least roughly true, something remarkable must have been happening. We know there were epidemics in Boston, and there was relatively little immigration; nevertheless the birth rate exceeded the death rate. Elsewhere in New England the population was doubling by natural increase in something less than every thirty years. Boston's population was probably not growing at this rate, but it must have been growing nevertheless. Then why was there no increase in the observable numbers? Far from absorbing and destroying part of the surplus population of the surrounding countryside as the English cities were doing, Boston seems to have been exporting people to the adjacent region. Its population was spreading into the near suburbs (Dorchester, Charlestown, Roxbury, and Boston have been described as a single bay area community throughout the colonial period), but it must have been spreading even more widely than that. How far afield Bostonians went we do not know: the record linkages needed to trace the exoduses into the countryside have not yet been worked out. But it seems likely that Boston's role in population development was almost the opposite of that of the major European cities: it seems to have been a nursery, not a graveyard, especially if, as has been suggested, there was a sharp increase in transient job seekers coming into Boston from the countryside after the mid-eighteenth century. Its capacity to absorb and redistribute large groups of new arrivals was severely limited.[9]

Philadelphia performed a different demographic function. How many immigrants entered the port of Philadelphia we do not know: certainly far more than the seventy thousand Germans known to have arrived before Independence. Yet while Philadelphia's population increased more than six and a half times in those years, reaching approximately thirty thousand in 1774, the city did not permanently absorb the majority of the immigrants, or even a very large part of that influx. Most of the immigrants who survived the transatlantic passage, the long dockside delays (longest for those in the worst physical condition), and the lethal "seasoning" period in the new disease environment eventually left the city and settled elsewhere. They spread out to the countryside, scattering west and south into southern Pennsylvania, western Maryland, and the backcountry of Virginia, settling where employment was available, or where kin or sect associations created natural communities for them, or where land was obtainable for use or purchase, or simply where the available routes of transportation led most easily. But this unfocused, uncoordinated distribution system was far from efficient. All sorts of difficulties of communication and transportation had to be overcome before the new arrivals could be absorbed into the countryside. As a result, most of the immigrants lived, often for substantial periods of time, in Philadelphia, and so that city developed what has been called a human warehousing capacity.[10]

At any given moment the city had hundreds of recently arrived and largely destitute newcomers in transit to more permanent locations. On the eve of the Revolution, for example, when the German Society in Philadelphia was trying to raise money for a building to house the incoming German immigrants, the Widow Kreiderin, according to the *Wöchentliche Pennsylvanische Staatsbote*, was putting up fifty to sixty redemptioners who were looking for the means to pay for their passages; the Widow Meyers was prepared to release the families she was housing to anyone who could pay their "freight" (transatlantic fare); and Martin Noll, at the upper end of Second Street, was still hoping somehow to unload the immigrants he had taken in, six months after they had arrived.[11] The ravages of this "warehousing," in terms of human suffering, were severe. The city's death rate, owing to the mortality among the new arrivals and to the diseases they brought with them and communicated to the natives, was extremely high; only an even more remarkable birth rate, in this youthful population, offset these losses. And there was a permanent and constantly renewed stratum of poverty that otherwise would not have existed. Indeed, the question is not why the poverty level rose in the middle and later years of the eighteenth century but why it remained as low as it did. Despite these costs, somehow, through most of the colonial period, the city's special warehousing function continued to operate and to characterize this community uniquely.[12]

New York too, though to a lesser extent, had a warehousing function, not mainly for Germans but for Scots and Scotch-Irish. But that city was also, and for immigrants primarily, a staging area managed directly or indirectly by land speculators; and of that function we know a good deal. While in New England there were innumerable children of prolific families in settled townships available to populate the backcountry and the near borderlands, in New York efforts had to be made to import people from abroad to settle the vast upcountry territory, and they arrived inevitably through New York City.

Intricately related lines of migration reaching from the British Isles to the upper Hudson and Mohawk valleys—from Loch Lomond to Lake Otsego; from Fort William, on Loch Linnhe, to Fort Edward, on the Hudson; from the Cairngorms to the Catskills; and from Frankfurt am Main to Frankfort on the Mohawk—came together on the docks of the East River. There immigrants, unloaded from ships arriving from everywhere in the Protestant world, especially from Scotland and Ireland, were quickly reached by sharp-eyed merchants and real-estate agents in touch with upcountry land speculators, and negotiations began. The indigent had little choice; they became tenants on wilderness land, or drifted into the city's labor force. But most were not entirely indigent and to some extent were able to consider options. When they could manage to do so, they sent agents up the Hudson to scout out the lands available for rent or sale. By the eve of the Revolution new arrivals were inspecting land as far north as the Canadian end of Lake Champlain and as far west as Lake Oneida, thirty miles from Lake Ontario.

The key figures in all of these maneuvers of the peopling process in New York were the New York City merchants, linked on the one hand to shippers and merchants in the British Isles and on the other to land speculators up north. Certain of the merchants—the DeLanceys, for example, and the colony secretary Goldsbrow Banyar, and the hustling attorney general John Tabor Kempe—had dual roles, as New York merchants and as upcountry land speculators. Occasionally the more enterprising inland real-estate operators worked through regular paid agents in the city: lesser merchants like the newly arrived Yorkshireman, John Wetherhead, for example, who in the 1770s served Sir William Johnson, the Mohawk land baron, as a scout for potential land purchasers among the new immigrants. Year after year the flow of arrivals to the East River docks continued, and was largely channeled up into the inland wilderness, to settle, ultimately, on uncultivated land hundreds of miles from the coast.[13]

It was a variegated, dynamic world. No simple pattern seems to fit any part of it. In the mid-seventeenth century the German engraver Merian published a celebrated work in many volumes depicting graphically the appearance of over two thousand German villages, towns, and cities. They are wonderful pictures—full of surprising details and vivid scenes. But one is struck by how similar these many communities were—similar in location, internal organization, street pattern. If a Merian had depicted the colonial American communities, he would have had to show a far more varied set of scenes, reflecting a far more diverse set of functions performed by these communities, to fit properly the highly differentiated pattern of life in this quickly developing world.[14]

The greatest source of variety lay in the ethnic and cultural composition of the incoming groups. The population that spread inland from coastal nodes to form new communities was a composite of ethnic and religious groups—Germans, French, Swiss, Scotch, Scotch-Irish, English, Caribbean islanders, Africans, Afro-Americans —carrying with them different cultural baggage, different patterns of family organization and discipline, different ways of working and living together. What has been called the "hybridisation of the various cultural groups . . . attracted to Penn's colony" was nothing unique to Pennsylvania; it took place everywhere south of New England—and in New England too, to a lesser extent, after the mid-eighteenth century. In southeastern Pennsylvania, Ulstermen and Scots followed Germans, who followed English and Welsh. Other, similar sequences occurred elsewhere—in western Maryland, in the part of New York that would become Vermont, in the Shenandoah Valley, in the backcountry of North and South Carolina, in the Georgia settlements along the Savannah River. And as these many groups spread through the backcountry and settled in growing inland communities and on farms and plantations scattered over millions of acres, complex regional configurations developed, which became in turn settings for later arrivals who filled in the interstices, thereby further complicating the emerging society. There was no single "American" pattern of family and community organization. There were many patterns, reflecting the variety of human sources from which the population had been recruited and the swiftly changing, fluid situations in which the people lived.[15] All was movement, change, growth, dispersal—and all was impelled forward by two powerful forces, two dynamic impulses that lay behind the entire peopling process.

Which brings me to my third proposition.

Proposition Three

After the initial phase of colonization, the major stimuli to population recruitment and settlement were, first, the continuing need for labor, and, second, land speculation. There were, as a result, two overlapping but yet distinctly different migration processes in motion throughout these years. Both linked America to Europe and Africa in a highly dynamic relationship and together account for much of the influx of people. But they drew on different socioeconomic groups and involved different modes of integration into the society. And land speculation shaped a relationship between the owners and the workers of the land different from that which prevailed in Europe.

As I suggested earlier, the original recruitment of the seventeenth-century population was largely, though not wholly, the product of efforts to divert to the colonies a portion of the mobile English labor force. Reliable estimates of the numbers involved have now been established: 378,000 emigrants from England to the Western Hemisphere in the course of the seventeenth century, of whom 155,000 went to the mainland colonies, the majority of them indentured servants. And we know something of their geographical origins. Almost all of the indentured servants came from southern England, with a high concentration in the Thames Valley, centered in

London. Their social origins are less clear, but there are fairly clear boundaries. These seventeenth-century labor migrants form a spectrum from the utterly destitute, the disreputable, and the vagrant, to respectable young artisans or would-be artisans seeking more secure employment and eventually an independent stake in the land. Cheap labor, these servants—young men predominantly, but women as well—formed the numerical basis of the white North American population south of New England.[16]

They continued to arrive, in reduced numbers, in the eighteenth century, but now as part of a more complex pattern of labor recruits. In these later years of the colonial period their numbers were supplemented by convicts from all over Britain: about fifty thousand of them were transported to America to serve out their time in unpaid labor along with the "free" indentured servants. There were Irish and Scotch too among the eighteenth-century labor recruits, and above all a mass of German redemptioners, whose presence, like that of the Irish, was a major fact of social life everywhere in North America, from Lunenburg in Nova Scotia to the southern borderlands of Georgia and Florida. But in the eighteenth century the newly recruited labor force was not only more complex in its social and geographical origins than it had been in the seventeenth; it was also—despite the number of convicts—more skilled, more sophisticated, and more respectable. Conditions in America had changed. Slaves had taken over much of the brute labor in the fields and elsewhere, and the demand for labor concentrated in a few major industries: iron manufacture, shipbuilding, construction work of all kinds—carpentry, masonry, glazing, metalwork, coach building—and textile manufacturing and distribution; and in the great range of service trades necessary for the increasingly affluent colonial communities.[17]

In page after page of the many extant letterbooks of the eighteenth-century merchants involved in labor recruitment, the need for skills, and not merely brute labor, is spelled out—specified down to the last detail. "The more weavers, shoemakers, tailors, joiners, carpenters, bricklayers, and farmers and the fewer women there are among them the better," one Maryland factor wrote in 1774. One customer needed a servant to help on the farm, but not any farm laborer who happened to turn up: he wanted, he said, "a westcountryman, that has been used to driving an ox team and understands cattle grazing and mowing grass. . . . I would chuse him middleaged." But though almost any skill could be used and its possessors' labor could be sold profitably in the American market towns, the greatest need was for workers who could build things—build almost anything: houses, bridges, fences, furniture, walls, roofs, carriages; who could repair things; and who could otherwise assist in maintaining the physical world of the maturing mainland colonies. So carpenters, joiners, masons, cartwrights, millwrights, wheelwrights, plasterers, braziers, pewterers, bricklayers, glaziers, and smiths of all kinds were in the highest demand and fetched the best prices in the labor markets scattered throughout the land. Send men, not women, the American middlemen wrote their correspondents in Britain; send young people, not old; and if the necessary skills are not available, send bright young boys, untrained but quick and intelligent— "likely sound young men & boys"—who could pick up the required skills in short order.[18]

The labor market was thus fundamentally different, for freemen, in the eighteenth century from what it had been in the seventeenth, and the response was visible in the social character of the newly arriving indentees. In the early years of settlement, one authority writes,

it is foolish to suppose that many persons of stable position in England would come to the colonies as servants. . . . The majority of servants would naturally be more or less worthless individuals who drifted to the colonies as a last resort, who were kicked out of England by irate fathers or expelled by the machinery of Bridewell and Newgate. These were the servants who had to be whipped for idleness, who ran away, committed thefts, and disturbed the peace. . . . There can be no doubt that towards the end of the colonial period better servants came, and the large migrations of 1773 did not bring nearly as much riff-raff, proportionately, as did the smaller movements of a century before. . . . The point was, of course, that the colonies had settled down into a stable existence; men could go there not as on a wild gamble, but with fair certainty of making a decent and even a comfortable living. It had become a reasonable project for the sober and industrious farmer, or the ambitious laborer.

On the eve of the Revolution 56 percent of the indentured servants arriving from England and Scotland claimed to

have the skills of trained artisans, and almost 20 percent of these many artisans—10 percent of all the indentured servants—described themselves as skilled in high-
precision or semi-artistic crafts. They claimed to be
goldsmiths, backgammon-table makers, bookbinders,
harpsichord makers, watch-movement makers, engravers,
glassblowers, lapidaries, mathematical-instrument makers, letter founders, sword cutters, gilders, paperhangers,
picture-frame makers.[19]

These tens of thousands of workers from the British
Isles and the continent of Europe to the mainland North
American colonies—simple laborers in the seventeenth
century, increasingly artisans and experienced farmworkers in the eighteenth—entered the society in a distinctive
way. Unpaid laborers for a number of years, they were
kept by their indentures from marriage, hence kept, temporarily but significantly, from contributing to the increase of the population. Restricted too as consumers,
they were immobilized geographically—all, that is, except the estimated 5 percent who escaped their bondage
and disappeared into the population at large. A potent
and cheap labor force at the height of its physical powers,
these indentured servants were important contributors to
the economy's productivity, but they were delayed
recipients of its bounty. And few of them contributed,
during their years as bondsmen, to the opening of
the land, which was peculiarly the work of the other
great segment of new arrivals in pre-Revolutionary America—settlers recruited by the land speculators, large and
small.

. . .

In discussing land speculation I trespass on the historical domain of Frederick Jackson Turner, who saw in pre-Revolutionary America a frontier world inhabited by farmers struggling with absentee bankers and land operators searching ruthlessly for profits—speculators who kept the workers of the land in financial bondage, withheld from use vast tracts of valuable land, and limited investments in public services in areas that were finally opened up. This image of the colonial past, elaborated by two generations of historians following in Turner's wake —Lois Mathews, Curtis Nettels, Louis Hacker, Roy Akagi, Ray Billington, and almost every textbook writer for half a century—appears now to be altogether misleading. Since at least 1955, when Charles Grant published his essay on land speculation in the frontier town of Kent, Connecticut, it has become clear that on almost every point Turner's formulation is mistaken as applied to the pre-Revolutionary years.[20]

Land speculation—the acquisition of land not for its use but for its resale value as a commodity in a rising market—was no special activity of absentee capitalists in the colonial period, and the western settlements were no agrarian preserves unsullied by commerce. Speculative commercial operations had been part and parcel of the settling of the earliest North American villages—of the founding of the very first Puritan New England towns, as well as those that followed in the eighteenth century.[21] It was never a special preserve of absentee capitalists.

A universal occupation from the beginning, land speculation was "the most common means of making a fortune in the colonies," as Aubrey Land explained two decades ago, and it accounts for "the most spectacular successes" enjoyed by the Chesapeake planters. It was engaged in, on a massive scale, by great landowners like the Earl of Granville, the Lords Baltimore, and Lord Fairfax, whose enormous holdings, larger than many of the sovereign states of Germany, came to them accidentally, by inheritance from an earlier and very different world; by wily British adventurers like Henry McCulloh and George Clarke, who managed through infinitely complicated tangles of Anglo-American manipulation and influence to claim large segments of American land; by recently arrived American residents of some resources —Alexander Spotswood, Daniel Dulany, Dr. Charles Carroll—who gradually accumulated large estates of wild land in areas they were familiar with; by established planters like the Byrds and the Carters, who added acre to acre and farm to farm, to accumulate huge holdings; by political insiders like Governor Fletcher's cronies in New York, whose loyalties were repaid by grants that, on paper at least, constituted whole counties, veritable kingdoms of uncultivated land[22]—but not only by such as these. Land speculation was everyone's work and it affected everyone, for it was a natural and rational response to two fundamental facts of American life: the extraordinarily low ratio of people to arable land, and the strong likelihood that the ratio would change quickly and radically as the population grew.

Every farmer with an extra acre of land became a land speculator—every town proprietor, every scrambling tradesman who could scrape together a modest sum for investment. Charles Grant put the point perfectly after examining with amazement some six thousand land transactions in the first twenty-two years of Kent, Connecticut's obscure history: "the humblest pioneers were apparently speculating their heads off."[23]

There was never a time in American history when land speculation had not been a major preoccupation of ambitious people. Within a single generation of the first settlements, the acquisition of land had taken on a new form and a new purpose; speculation in land futures was fully launched as a universal business, and it developed quickly. By 1675, politically influential individuals in Massachusetts had been granted personal gifts by the legislature totaling 130,000 acres, in parcels far larger than any conceivable personal use could justify and beyond any possible personal use by their children or grandchildren. The members of the Dudley Council acquired, in a series of land deals between 1660 and 1689, almost 400,-000 acres, over half of which was claimed by one individual, Richard Wharton.[24] During the same years, in the Chesapeake region, small planters had become large planters by virtue of land accumulations as a new breed of planter-entrepreneur learned how to amass headrights and how to translate these claims first into warrants and then into actual titles to large parcels of unoccupied land.[25] By the 1690s, when Governor Fletcher of New York was handing out princely largesse to his political allies, the use of political influence, both in the colonies and in London, to establish titles to wild land had become common everywhere, and land speculation was shaping the peopling of the land.

What lay behind this ubiquitous enterprise was, of course, the belief that as population increased, wild territory would become cultivated, and land values would soar. The first step was to establish one's claim; and the prodigies of effort devoted to that end are among the most remarkable facts of early American life. But that was only the first step. The second, upon which everything else in the end depended, was to populate the land one claimed; and to accomplish that, efforts were made whose consequences were crucial to the peopling of America.

The strategies used by land speculators to people their lands, and the techniques they devised to realize actual profits from the settlers once they arrived, were as ingenious as they were various. The simplest approach was to locate one's claim where settlers seemed likely to appear, and then to encourage them to settle by attractive offers. Some active guidance, some forceful promotion in the form of advertisement or actual contracts with communities seeking relocation, was usually needed to direct the settlers to the proper spot. The careful guidance by land speculators of people already in motion or easily moved accounts for the settlement of whole regions of the backcountry, generation after generation. A map of such settlements could be drawn for the whole area east of the Mississippi, and the routes of population movements depicted, showing the role of American land speculators in directing the flow of domestic migrations.[26]

There were great successes; but it was a tricky business, and there were many failures. Excessive greed could easily backfire, for settlers in motion could in the end move elsewhere, or simply defy the landowners' financial demands in these backlands where constabularies were nonexistent. So a band of New York land operators, scrambling to establish claims in the Mohawk Valley where a community of Germans was known to be settling, forced those immigrants to scatter and move in small groups through the backcountry, most of them to settle eventually in Pennsylvania.[27]

Though the shrewdest, or luckiest, of the speculators profited simply by taking out claims to land located in the path of domestic population flows or were able to attract to their land local migrants already in motion, most were obliged to take more active steps to people the land they claimed. From the start, American land speculators looked to European sources of population for the settlers they needed and reached overseas to recruit them. Together with the shippers who profited by transporting the immigrants,[28] they became thereby dynamic forces propelling forward the peopling of the land.

One day their efforts will be fully depicted: the documentation exists for recording a great many of the hundreds of efforts made by speculators to settle immigrants on the lands they claimed. Their enterprises help explain the complicated patchwork pattern of immigrant settlements over large areas. These were enterprises that involved complex international maneuvering through agents and subagents in an era of extremely poor communication and rudimentary management facilities. Wherever one looks in the eighteenth century one finds individuals and groups arranging privately for the importation of people from abroad and seeking to locate them on lands they could claim. As one probes these myriad maneuvers one finds tendrils snaking over thousands of miles and through complicated tangles of intrigue, to produce in the end some palpable increment to the British North American population.

So Samuel Waldo, a Boston merchant, got control of extensive lands in Maine east of the Kennebec River and began an elaborate effort to populate them with immigrants. In 1742 he managed to import a shipload of Germans through the agency of one Sebastian Zouberbühler, who was otherwise engaged in managing domestic German population movements. Interest spread, and by 1750 the government of Massachusetts, supported by Waldo and the Kennebec land company and convinced of the need to follow Pennsylvania in recruiting settlers from abroad to populate the exposed border areas, joined in the immigration business.

The government, together with the speculators, engaged the assistance of two agents: an unscrupulous German-born Pennsylvania shopkeeper, Joseph Crellius, at that time carrying on various dubious operations in Germany; and a high-minded imperial official and printer of Frankfurt am Main, Heinrich Ehrenfried Luther, to speed on the recruitment. Within two years a large bubble of enterprise developed, involving the two agents, a clutch of subagents operating on a price-per-head basis as "newlanders" or *Werber* in the Rhineland, and at least seven shipping firms in Rotterdam and four in Amsterdam fighting for pieces of the profits. A complicated network spread throughout the river system of the upper Rhineland, managed at various headquarters in counting houses, inns, and private houses in Speyer, Heilbron, Frankfurt, and the two Dutch ports, all of it tied in, in some subtle fashion, with the powerful government-connected Anglo-American merchant house of Christopher Kilby and Company.

Waldo, who was the original force behind all of this, suddenly appeared in Germany, proclaiming himself a "Royal British Captain [and] hereditary lord of Broad Bay, Massachusetts," and advertising splendid terms to all who would return with him to what were supposed to be his ancestral lands in Maine. His and Massachusetts's *Werber*, knowing a good thing when they saw it, then went seriously to work. They picked up every footloose vagabond they could find, bamboozled respectable families by fancy enticements, and packed off several hundred "freights," as they referred to fare-paying adult immigrants, to rallying points along the Rhine, whence they were relayed, under increasingly sordid conditions, to the Dutch shippers, who reduced even the more affluent of them to beggary before sending them on to New England.

Then the bubble burst. By 1753 the German agents were locked in combat, the shippers had become ruthless in their heightened competition, German officials had begun to crack down on this manipulated emigration of respectable taxpaying subjects, and the sponsors of the whole undertaking were facing bankruptcy as costs spiraled. The ultimate result was the arrival under the worst possible conditions of several hundred Germans, only a few of whom settled on the frontier as the government had intended. Most of them scattered along the Maine coast and into the near interior, where the speculators sought to extract the profits they had planned. Not all of the sixty families that Waldo personally conducted from Germany to Broad Bay (Waldoborough) survived a freezing winter in the shed he had prepared for their arrival, and only some of these survivors ultimately settled on his land. But however few they were, their presence —like that of the seventy or so Lowland Scots he also recruited—was the result of his haphazard entrepreneurship. The rampaging "speculative fever" that gripped the imaginations of the leading landowners and merchants of New England accounted for an array of such clusters of immigrant settlements scattered across northern New England.[29]

All of this is one minuscule example of a phenomenon that appeared throughout the length and breadth of British North America, with ramifications through broad reaches of Ireland, Britain, and continental Europe. So John Rea and George Galphin, Irish-born Indian traders in Georgia, joined with one Lachlan McGillivray to exploit the possibilities of land speculation by patenting land intended by Georgia for new border settlements and then importing, through relatives in Ireland, several hundred Irishmen. Their success stimulated others to patent land in the same area of Georgia in the hope of profitable sales or rentals to immigrants, and these speculators in turn found the need to do the recruiting themselves. Within a four-year period seven hundred Irishmen were added to the population of Georgia by their efforts, and this was one of a hundred such efforts taking place all over British North America—efforts which together account for most of the 33,000 Irish Protestants whose emigration to America in the fifteen years before Independence became such a serious concern of the British government.[30]

It was in part to prevent the depopulation of the British Isles by enterprising land speculators like these that the Privy Council in 1773 changed the policy that had hitherto governed the distribution of crown land in the colonies. No longer were the governors and their councils allowed to grant such land in unlimited quantities, accumulating large profits from fees. As of February 3, 1774, lands were to be distributed by sale, not by grant, and sold in officially surveyed plots, at public auctions and at published prices, with fees for passing the papers specified by the crown. The government had been driven to this radical change, John Pownall, the under-secretary of state for the colonies, explained, by the many complaints that had been received charging that the "great emigration of the inhabitants" was severely injuring "the landed interests, the commerce, and the manufactures of these kingdoms" and that those who were departing "may have been induced to such emigration by delusive proposals of encouragement which have been unwarrantably held out by persons who have obtained gratuitous grants of land in His Majesty's colonies in America." For that reason the colonial governors had been given "the most positive instructions not to pass any grants of land within their respective governments," then or in the future.[31]

So the British government in the end understood the relationship between speculation in American land and emigration from Britain. But the new policy had little effect, and in any case came too late. Land speculation was, and remained, boundless, ubiquitous. The Colden family of New York attempted by generous land grants to attract a stream of English and Scottish immigrants to their 45,000 acres in upstate New York, while at the same time Lord Adam Gordon, the land-poor younger son of a great Highland landlord, toured the colonies in 1764 and attempted to establish himself as a landlord in America (where he never intended to settle) by purchasing land for speculation in Florida and New York. Together with his kinsman the Duke of Atholl, Gordon set about recruiting settlers wherever he could find them in the British Isles, hoping to build a fortune by promoting emigration.[32] In this he was typical of many Scottish gentlemen who arrived to inspect frontier land just before the Revolution, and he exemplified one of the most revealing aspects of the whole enterprise of land speculation and population recruitment in the pre-Revolutionary period. For it is the British side of the picture that contains the most extreme examples of the speculative fever that gripped the Anglo-American world; it illustrates vividly some of the forces at play in this vital part of the peopling process.

The peace treaty of 1763 threw open a vast territory to settlement: two wilderness regions at the geographical extremities, Nova Scotia and the Floridas, and between them an enormous inland arc stretching from back-country Maine to upcountry New York and Vermont, to the Appalachian plateau in southwestern Pennsylvania, through the Great Valley of the Appalachians, to north-western North Carolina and eastern Tennessee, to up-country South Carolina, and across the Savannah River to the great new land cessions of northeastern Georgia. The precise dimensions of this newly available territory are not known, but certainly some tens of millions of acres were now open for exploitation, and the resulting frenzy of land speculation, closely related to population recruitment, in the decade after 1763 was at least as much a British event as it was an American.

Of all of the territory now open for fresh exploitation, it was the exotic deep south—especially the unknown Floridian lands that Coleridge would soon immortalize as Xanadu—it was this strange, semitropical mystery land, Spanish before 1763, that particularly gripped the imagination of people in Britain: people everywhere in Britain, in the provinces as well as in the metropolis. Enthusiasm was high even before the peace treaty was concluded. When the botanist John Bartram's first account of his travels in East Florida was published in 1766, the effect was stunning. Lord Adam Gordon reported in London:

it "has sett us all Florida mad." It sent men's ambitions reeling and stirred latent longings for the feudal past.[33]

Denys Rolle was one of the most rhapsodic of the dreamers, one of the richest, and one of the most energetic. His family had been the wealthiest landowners in Devonshire for a century, and the inheritor of all this wealth dreamed up his projects for Florida, which seem to have obsessed him, in Stevenstone House, his "fine old mansion" set in broad parkland well stocked with deer. He began in 1763 with a vision of a huge semifeudal proprietary colony which he located, on the crude maps then available, north of the Gulf of Mexico, deep inland, near the present Georgia-Florida-Alabama boundary. One of the settlements he thereafter dreamed of was to be established in the west of Florida, near present-day Tallahassee; the other in the east, near the Atlantic coastline. He blandly promised to connect the two by safe lines of communication he would construct through what was in fact two hundred miles of impassable wilderness. Later, frustrated by the squalid reality of the little plantation he personally founded in the jungles along the St. Johns River, he dreamed of an even greater estate, this time a swath of land approximately forty miles wide and one hundred miles long (hence two and a half million acres) stretching east from the Gulf of Mexico at Tampa Bay across almost the whole of the Florida peninsula. The colony—"one entire country"—was to be held of the crown by military tenure (he promised to put a thousand men into the field at the summons of the crown), to be peopled by the impoverished masses of Britain, who would there find refuge and rehabilitation, and to be governed, not by the "arbitrary" powers of justices of the peace appointed by petty-minded crown governors, but by the "ancient and known constitutions" of "county, hundred, and manor courts, with courts leet and courts baron."

Some of the grandest visions of Florida's future came from an even more remote region of Britain than Devonshire. In Monymusk House, a turreted mansion on the side of a lake twenty miles northwest of Aberdeen, Scotland, Sir Archibald Grant, the successful proprietor of a newly modernized estate of ten thousand acres, brooded on the huge territories in North America that Britain had acquired, and found his ambitions soaring. In March 1764 he confided his thoughts to his kinsman Sir Alexander Grant, Member of Parliament and a powerful London merchant. "Since ever I could read on these subjects," he wrote, "I have been convinced, and am daily more and more confirmed in opinion, that America will at a periode, I don't presume to say when, be the grand seat of Empire and all its concomitants." Everything pointed to America's future greatness: the soil there, the minerals, the navigation, and simply the "variable nature and constant rotation of human things." The opportunities now available in the new provinces were extraordinary: huge properties almost for the asking, small quit rents, forfeitures unlikely. Furthermore, and most important, he wrote, people were available for settlement. Every country, "and especially [the Scottish] highlands, have people [who are] ambitious, avaricious, or some how uneasy or whimsical"; most often they "ramble [off] to [the] army, or somewhere abroad"—and where better could they go than to Britain's own new colonies? He could personally guarantee one hundred families from Scotland "of sufficient substance to move and settle themselves, each of whom would carry some underlings with them—to manage sub-grants or leases." And it would be easy too, he wrote, to get people from Ireland, Germany, Switzerland, "Civenns [i.e., Cévennes] [and] Provenze." As to where to locate such a grant or grants, he favored going *both* north and south—both to cool climates and to warm: "2 strings to the bow is prudent." In the north he would recommend "something on either or both sides of the Bay of Fundy, especially on or near St. Johns River, and oposite to Hallifax or the Istmus [of Chignecto]." In the south "anywhere near Pensicola, Mobile, or the River Mississippi as high as Ohio might do very well."

So successful British landowners, squires of hundreds of acres, dreamed of far greater proprietary estates than they had ever actually seen, estates to be peopled by farming families from northern Europe, in a land they could scarcely imagine. Applications for the designated twenty-thousand-acre grants in Florida began arriving at the Board of Trade as soon as they could be legally received —but not from people likely to lead settlements themselves. The applications came from speculators with grand synoptic visions, which included Nova Scotia and the two Floridas, Quebec, and Georgia, as well as new acquisitions in the Caribbean.

Names already familiar, or soon to become familiar, in

land development in Nova Scotia appeared also as applicants for grants in the Floridas, principally East Florida. The Earl of Egmont, son of one of the founders of Georgia, was famous not only for his nostalgia for a feudal world long since vanished but for his "assiduous application in prosecution of any undertaking he embarks in." In the early 1760s he turned his "attention, precision, [and] method" to land acquisition in the mainland south as well as in the maritime north. In the same years that he advanced a notorious proposal to be created the feudal "Lord Paramount" of Prince Edward Island and was designing the "grand divisions" of his 22,000-acre estate near Halifax, Nova Scotia, he invested heavily in East Florida land.

He began as co-owner of an inland plantation which he hoped to settle as his family's estates in Ireland had been settled, "by younger sons of gentlemen, and tenants in England." When that failed, he concentrated his efforts on a slave plantation, of which he was "exceeding fond," on Amelia, or Egmont, Island, a thirteen-mile-long strip of land just off the Florida coast near the Georgia boundary; in all, Egmont established claims to 65,000 acres in East Florida. The Earl of Dartmouth managed to acquire grants totaling 100,000 acres covering the entire region of the present city of Miami and the shoreline of Biscayne Bay. Richard Oswald, the future negotiator of the American peace treaty of 1783—a Scot of great wealth, gained as a food contractor and general merchant during the Seven Years War—debated carefully whether he should invest in Nova Scotia or in East Florida or in both, before finally deciding on East Florida. Already a leading West Indian sugar planter and co-owner with Henry Laurens of a South Carolina plantation, he became one of the major absentee landowners in Florida.

Very few if any of these British land speculators (none of whom had the slightest intention of settling on their American properties) profited from their investments in these schemes. For, as Henry Laurens knew so well and tried so hard to convince others, successful land speculation required a minute knowledge of the land and a careful and continuing assessment of what kinds of people were likely to settle where. And it required above all a precise calculation of just when a landlord's mixture of demands and support would entice settlers and when it would drive them away. That complicated calculation— which involved the going rates for rents, the purchase price of land in the immediate region and in the other areas the settlers would be able to move to, and the cost of borrowing money—was almost impossible to make correctly by an absentee, especially an absentee with no personal knowledge of the condition of land in these parts of America, and often impossible to make even through a more or less reliable agent, which few of these grant planners ever had.

But they tried. Some formed small partnerships, some virtual syndicates devoted to organizing the shiploads of emigrants from Britain, from the Low Countries, from France, from the German states, from the Swiss cantons —from anywhere: from Leghorn in northern Italy, from islands in the Mediterranean, from the Peloponnesus, from Turkey. But the actual organizing, supplying, shipping, and settling of people on the land was difficult and expensive, and hence risky. Occasionally they hired brokers to do the job, with results reflected in this advertisement in the *Newcastle Journal* in April 1774. "Lands in *North-America,*" is the heading:

HENRY TAYLOR, broker, in North-Shields [the exit port of Newcastle], Northumberland, begs leave to acquaint those who are now leaving this country for America, that he is commissioned to sell several tracts of land in Nova Scotia, the Island of St. John's [Prince Edward Island], and most of the other provinces.

The proprietors of these estates, residing in England and having no connection with the colonies except their property in these lands, intend disposing of them at lower rates than such tracts can be bought at in the respective provinces.

"Copies of the plans of these estates," the advertisement concludes, "with accounts of their situations &c," may be obtained from Henry Taylor or from five named sub-agents, one located in Durham, three in the nearby North Riding of Yorkshire, and one in the city of Hull, in the East Riding.[34]

But these speculators and their brokers, thousands of miles from the land in question, were not likely to profit from direct sales. Most of them had little notion of what the basis of successful land speculation in North America had proved to be. For it had little in common with the process of profiting from sales of land in long-settled, long-cultivated areas of England, land that carried with it tenants and subtenants and whole populations of marginal workers. Most of the land of North America was wild, and there was no stable population of tenants. To recruit such rent-paying workers would require heavy investments to clear the land and build habitations, investments that would clearly be uneconomical: capital could be invested more profitably in other ways. But if the land remained wild, why should anyone rent it, especially if similar land lay all about, ready to be purchased and exploited? Far wiser than direct investment in preparing the land for profitable rentals and permanent tenancy was the capital formation, independent of the speculators' investments, created by the labor of the users of the land. If they were to be successful, speculators had quickly to see the strange wisdom of not attempting, at first, to sell the land at all, or even to rent it out profitably, but of letting it out at very low rent, or at no rent, to settlers who by their own labor would clear the land, break the soil to cultivation, and build at least rudimentary shelters. After this initial period of low or no rents, the land would have acquired a new value and could *then* be rented profitably or sold—and sold, often, to the very settlers whose initial rents had been paid in the form of labor and whose purchases could be financed by mortgage loans offered by the original speculators themselves. At the end of such a typical long-term transaction, the speculator would possess cultivated land in place of wild land or would have sold it either for immediate profit or for loan repayments which might extend over many years—all of this with little or no outlay of funds. And the tenant-turned-landowner would have obtained a farm, or the low-cost use of a farm, in exchange for the investment of his labor.[35]

The variations on this model, particularly attractive to immigrant settlers, took many forms, all of them ways of rendering wild land valuable with the minimum investment of actual funds. So in 1744 Daniel Dulany, Sr., bought "Tasker's Chance" along the Monocacy River in western Maryland, which lay on the route the Germans were taking into the Shenandoah Valley. In fact German squatters, unable to raise the money to buy the plot, were already on the site when Dulany bought it. He paid 5s 8d per acre for the seven thousand undeveloped acres, and quickly sold at a severe loss five thousand of them, in hundred- and five-hundred-acre parcels, to the local Germans and their friends in the surrounding area. But he knew what he was doing. The Germans' labor on the land they bought so enhanced the value of the remaining and adjoining two thousand acres which Dulany kept that he could sell that parcel at a profit (it went for over £1 per acre) that more than covered all his earlier losses. And further, as the population in the region increased by these devices, Dulany was able to sell the town lots in Frederick Town, which he founded in one corner of the tract in 1745, at a very substantial profit. Similarly, James Duane laid out Duanesburgh, on the Schoharie River near Schenectady, New York, by leasing or selling alternate farms only, "so that the improvements of the first comers would add value to the reserved plots." Like many other land developers, Duane omitted the rents altogether on lands he leased out, for the first five or ten years. Under these conditions farmers who could purchase often chose to rent, especially if the lessors were willing to provide at least some of such elementary facilities as sawmills, gristmills, schools, and roads.[36] The settlers created the speculators' profit by the investment of their labor, even if only in adjoining land. For them "tenancy" was a relationship that had acquired a new meaning.

There were, of course, lifetime tenants in the colonies, some in the seventeenth century, more in the late colonial period. Recent studies of the Pynchon family's control of real estate in seventeenth-century Springfield, Massachusetts, which reduced most of the town's farmers to tenants or dependents of one sort or another, and of the Calvert family's estates in Maryland reveal a degree of tenancy unsuspected before; and tenancy is now known to have spread significantly in Virginia as well. But the Pynchons' control of Springfield's land faded in the early eighteenth century, and what made the Maryland study possible was the documentation left behind when the Calverts, judging the time to be ripe, finally sold these rental properties.[37]

There were always individual landowners who intended to keep properties as permanent or semipermanent rentals, but the option to sell was always a dominant consideration and a sensible one; eventually almost all such properties changed hands. In most areas the economy was too fluid to justify perpetual rentals; land was too easily available, however limited it might be in specific areas at specific times; and mobility was too vital a part of the entire social and economic situation to make possible a re-creation of the stable pattern of *rentiers* and tenants that lay at the heart of traditional landed society.

At any given time there were many tenants in certain areas of colonial America, but the meaning of that fact is not revealed by a static cross-sectional description. A large proportion of the tenants at any given time were recent immigrants or farmers who chose to rent when they might have bought. The meaning of tenancy in the American situation lies in the overall career patterns of individual tenants and the histories of the lands they worked. Such longitudinal histories—of people's lives and of the successive uses of particular plots of land—reveal, not the gradual re-creation of traditional forms but a new and dynamic process that was a central force in the peopling of America.

The need for a labor force and the imperatives of land speculation—these were major forces at work behind the population recruitment through these years; and while they overlapped in their influence, they were yet distinct, and created in effect a dual migration. The labor recruiters drew into the peopling process elements of the working class, chiefly from the south of England, to a lesser extent from the Scottish Highlands and Protestant Ireland. Occasionally their recruits were the utterly dispossessed, the indigent, the homeless, broken victims of a remorseless economic system. More often they were underemployed, frustrated, fearful, but still enterprising young artisans, journeymen, and casually employed workers—workers who were more or less trained, still young and unmarried, and hence highly mobile; some of them deliberately chose to be indentured as a strategy for making their way.

The land speculators, too, attracted the underemployed poor, but more often they drew in families, often sizable families of some small substance, hit by rent increases that threatened their future security, resentful of personal services they were still required to perform, and eager for a fresh start as landowners or at least tenants of independent status capable of expressing their energies in expansive ways. Some of these families were surprisingly affluent, but rich or poor, by liquidating their property, in part or in full, they could pay for their families' unencumbered entry into the new world, buy or rent a stake in the land, equip themselves for the work that lay ahead, and tide themselves over the lean period before the first crops could be produced. Many of these free families were destined to be frontiersmen in each successive generation. Consumers from the start, they were producers too, and prolific contributors to the rapidly increasing population.

III

A Domesday Book
for the Periphery

I n the years 1085–1087 William I, the Conqueror, sought to gain administrative control of the England he had just conquered; he sought too to establish a basis for wide-scale taxing; and he hoped also, and more generally (as the Anglo-Saxon Chronicle put it), to discover how the "land . . . was peopled, and with what sort of men." In order to do all this, William sent out teams of investigators—*legati*—to collect from every shire, hundred, and vil a description of the new territory. The information was digested into land records known as Domesday Book—and looking over those extraordinary documents in their modern reconstruction by H. C. Darby, I wondered:

Suppose William III— like the first William, a foreigner who, in 1689, had come from across the channel to assume the throne of England and who knew precious little about his new realm, and its extension overseas in North America—suppose he had done the same. Suppose he had set out to survey his empire in North America as of, say, 1700. And suppose, fur-

ther, that he had wanted not only a record of land tenures but also a social description of North America as it then existed, and to accomplish this had sent out teams of legati to report on this great territory in four large circuits.

And suppose, finally, beyond all that, and more important, that he had instructed these legati not only to report on their own circuits as they found them but to compare notes with each other and see if there were any qualities or characteristics common to all of these regions.

None of this is altogether improbable. We know that William was well aware of the importance of the American colonies, if only because of their role in his military and diplomatic campaign against France. We know too that he understood their indirect contribution to the tax sources of the nation. And we know that he personally made decisions in colonial matters.

Suppose, therefore, that he had done all this. What would the result have been? What would such a Domesday Book, cultural and social as well as tenurial, have looked like? What would the four legati have reported?

In each of the areas these *legati* would have found developments under way that fundamentally shaped the emerging local characteristics of early American culture. But in addition, and more important, they would have found a strange common element running through all of these regions, a peculiar quality that persisted in the generations that followed. This common characteristic could not have been found in an earlier age; and at any later stage it would seem immutable, too deeply set, too elaborately interwoven into the general fabric of society, to be clearly identified. The crucial phase of origins lay in these transition years at the turn of the century—a soft, plastic moment of history when what would become familiar and obvious to later generations was just emerging, unsurely, from a strange and unfamiliar past.

Change was everywhere, together with confusion and controversy. The *legati* in the first circuit, New England, would have reported an agonizing transformation, impelled by the inmost tendencies of a highly self-conscious and cultivated religious culture and by the buffeting of external events. They would have found a Puritan world whose inner spirit, once powerfully creative and fearless, had survived into a third generation in a faded and defensive form. The fierce religious intensity, the sense of daring and risky enterprise in the service of a demanding God—an enterprise of great relevance to the whole informed Protestant world—all of that had passed. The first generation's accomplishments had been products of passionate striving in an atmosphere of fear and desperation; but to their children the founders' world was an inheritance they were born into—respected but familiar and routine. And to *their* children, adults at the end of the century, what had once been rebellious, liberating, and challenging had become a problematic anachronism.

So John Winthrop, Jr., a second-generation Puritan, physician, amateur scientist, and imaginative entrepreneur, lived out his life in backwoods Connecticut struggling to maintain contact with the larger world from which his parents had dared to escape. He wrote letter after letter to the Royal Society in London, of which he was the first American member, in an effort to keep in touch. He sent over scientific specimens, anything he could get hold of—rattlesnake skins, birds' nests, plants, crabs, strange pigs. He studied the Society's *Transactions* so as not to fall too far behind. And to those concerned with the propagation of the Gospel he dispatched John Eliot's Algonquian translation of the Bible and two essays written in Latin by Indian students at Harvard. But these were failing efforts. In the end loneliness and isolation overcame him. He died, venerated in the villages along the Connecticut River—themselves changing like autumn leaves from vital, experimental religious communities to sere, old-fashioned backwoods towns—but forgotten in the greater world at home. His sons, however, provincial land speculators and petty politicians, had no such memories as their father had had, and no such aspirations; they suffered, therefore, no such disappointments. They were altogether native to the land, and their cultural horizons had narrowed to its practical demands.

The third generation, adults at the end of the century, were dull, rather rustic provincials, whose concerns had little to do with the spiritual yearnings and ascetic self-discipline of their grandparents. Their interests centered on much more mundane matters—on the struggle to profit from their farms, on the conduct of trade; above all, on the consequences of extraordinary population growth.[1]

The New England population—self-enclosed, lacking in significant accretions from abroad—was growing, in the seventeenth century, at a rate of 2.6 or 2.7 percent in a year, hence doubling every twenty-seven years. This phenomenal growth was no consequence of a peculiarly high birth rate—New England and old England scarcely differed in this—but of a low death rate, the result not of the absence of epidemics but of their low intensity, which allowed swift demographic recoveries. This regional population growth and low mortality rate—which declined in the eighteenth century—had the effect of propelling the boundaries of Anglo-American settlements out from the original coastal and riverbank enclaves. By the early eighteenth century, a settlement map would show a pattern surprisingly like the Soviet crossed hammer and sickle, the sickle being a fifty-mile-wide band of British settlements south along the coast from New Hampshire around the Cape to the New York boundary, the hammer being the northern penetration of settlement up the Connecticut River—a solid arm two or three townships wide, reaching inland straight up from Long Island Sound north to the level of Brattleboro, Vermont. Between 1660 and 1710, 209 new townships had been settled in New England, an average of over four per year.[2]

Behind this remarkable spread of settlement lay the central mechanism at work in this northernmost circuit of the turn-of-the-century Domesday survey. In any newly established New England town, founding families were able to subdivide their land to the satisfaction of at most only two successive generations. The fourth, sometimes even the third, generation felt a relative land shortage, or rather a land hunger created by their expectations, which led some to venture out into new settlements, often on land earlier invested in, speculatively, by far-sighted kin. There is no absolute lower boundary of acreage per child that marks the point at which a family broke out of its original location. Some sent representatives out soon after their establishment; some managed to maintain four generations in the original community by the comprehensive utilization of the family's initial properties. But the common experience was for families to reach out to newly opening territory in the third or fourth generation, when some kind of threshold of optimal town population and maximal morselization of land was reached—optimal and maximal in terms of certain widely shared expectations.[3]

None of this concern with population growth and land distribution—any more than with local trade and overseas commerce—was felt to be incompatible with the restrained and serious way of life instinctive to these third-generation provincial Puritans. But, combined with the cooling of religious passion, it shifted the tone and quality of New England culture in fundamental ways. New England was culturally and ethnically a homogeneous world, derived from a single period of English emigration, 1630–1640, spreading out quickly, westward and northward, into uncultivated lands and forming a network of communities set in forest clearings and natural meadowland and linked by hundreds of footpaths, by rough, stump-filled horse-and-wagon trails, and by river routes. In these isolated but associated communities lived a population of austere and prolific country folk, pious without passion, ambitious for worldly things, yet still attuned, in some degree, to the appeal of their ancestors' spiritual quests, still aware of, and to some extent unified by, a distinctive cultural heritage.

No such homogeneity would have been found in the area of the second circuit. It was a remarkably different world. In the settlements scattered from the Hudson River south to the Delaware, the legates would have found ethnic diversity of the most extreme kind, and not a single expanding network of communities impelled outward by the dynamics of a distinctive demographic process, but half a dozen different demographic processes moving in different phases at different speeds.

Small migrant flows over many years had produced New York's population of 1700. Originally people had come from the Netherlands; then, in small numbers, from New England, from England, from France, from the German principalities, from Brazil, indirectly from Africa, and from Virginia and Maryland. Still only slowly growing, the colony of only eighteen thousand souls was a mosaic of groups, ill-integrated and often hostile to each other. In the Hudson Valley there were Dutch, French, Walloons, Palatines, and English. Manhattan, with a population of only five thousand, was dominated numerically by the Dutch but politically, socially, and economically by the English and French; it had a small community of Jews and a sizable group—

perhaps as much as 15 percent of the population—of Africans, almost all of them slaves. And the religious scene was even more complex than the ethnic, and had been from the colony's earliest years. "Here," Governor Dongan reported in 1687, "bee not many of the Church of England, [and] few Roman Catholicks, [but] abundance of Quakers—preachers, men and women, especially—singing Quakers, ranting Quakers, Sabbatarians, Anti-sabbatarians, some Anabaptists, some Independants, some Jews; in short, of all sorts of opinions there are some, and the most part of none at all."[4]

Elsewhere in this middle circuit the ethnic complexity was similar. The Jerseys had been settled by widely differing groups entering from different directions. Originally Dutch from Manhattan and New Englanders had settled in the northeast of the colony; then English Quakers began the occupancy of West Jersey, approaching from the Delaware River in the southwest. Some Swedes, long established on the Delaware, moved east to the Atlantic coastal plain; and hundreds of Scots—clients of the Scottish East Jersey proprietors—settled a hopeful new capital at Perth Amboy, an excellent harbor opposite the tip of Staten Island, and then fanned out in an inland arc, joining in with New Englanders and Dutch to populate, in the 1680s, a series of poly-ethnic settlements in the Raritan Valley. Only a few original settlements of New Englanders and Dutch in the northeast remained ethnically homogeneous.

Pennsylvania's diversity was similar. By 1700 the settlements there, expanding back westward from the Delaware River, filled out the whole southeastern corner of the colony, and throughout that large area, as in New Jersey and New York, settlement had advanced without central organization or control, creating a mosaic whose pattern was formed simply by ease of routes of access, accidents of land claims, and the contours of the terrain.

This whole middle circuit of British North America, founded by diverse peoples from all over the American colonies, and from Britain, western Europe, and West Africa, was the scene of continuous contention: Dutch vs. Anglo-French; Scots vs. English; Quakers vs. Quakers. The worst struggle was in New York City. There the animosities between numerically dominant Dutch and the politically and economically dominant Anglo-French had led to a violent upheaval—Leisler's Rebellion—that tore the colony apart in 1691 and was only temporarily resolved two years later by the judicial murder of the ringleaders. In 1700 that fierce politico-ethnic struggle, whose origins lay deep in the peopling process, was still the dominant fact in the colony's public life, though it was beginning to fade and to reshape into a new configuration.

Pennsylvania too had had turmoils rooted in political and ethnic diversity. William Penn, harassed at every turn and frustrated in his hopes for a tranquil, well-structured society in Pennsylvania, cursed and cursed again what he called these "scurvy quarrels that break out to the disgrace of the Province." And so too did a succession of governors in the other colonies of this region, who struggled to maintain public authority and a modicum of community spirit and social order in widely scattered settlements of different peoples, living, often, in primitive conditions.

It was a strange, disorderly world, the commissioners for the second circuit would have had to report—lacking anything like a uniform land system; lacking social cohesion; and chaotic in public affairs to the point of political violence. Yet, amid all this diversity and turmoil a more coherent world was emerging, with something of the normal hierarchy of statuses and wealth, if not of rank, which in traditional societies reinforced private as well as public order. In New York a small provincial aristocracy of sorts was taking stable form. It was largely Anglo-French in origins, though it included significant Dutch elements too. Based on political and economic privilege, it was just then, at the turn of the century, being secured by a series of spectacular land grants along the Hudson and on Long Island, grants that had been and still were being hotly contested, but would soon be solidly confirmed. The Dutch dominated only the upriver center at Albany, with its monopoly of the Indian trade, but the leaders there were doubly provincial: gentry on the outer frontier of a frontier world. And in Pennsylvania too a leadership group was emerging from the confusion of the settling years—Quaker merchants for the most part, together with a few Anglicans who arrived with some capital and connections throughout the Atlantic trading world and who knew how to turn political advantage to economic profit.[5]

But if these were provincial aristocracies, they were

still supple, still without the full external attributes of superiority, their distinction still well within the range of competition by ambitious but disadvantaged natives and by well-connected or prosperous newcomers.

Something of the same development was overtaking the world of the third circuit, the Chesapeake colonies—but at a different pace, and emerging out of entirely different demographic circumstances. There a transformation was underway that would affect the entire course of American history, and the history of the Western world indirectly.

The population history of the tobacco country of Virginia and Maryland, the commissioners would have discovered, had two, but only two, characteristics in common with that of New England: its white population was largely derived from English sources, and its numbers, at the time of the survey, were approximately the same as those of the Puritan colonies. But the number of immigrants that had arrived, the timing of their arrival, and their social, physical, and legal condition had been entirely different. New England's original immigration had taken place in a single short span of years early in the century; these Puritan immigrants and their followers had settled in a temperate and healthy environment; and they had been overwhelmingly free people, not bound servants, and organized for the most part in family groups, with only a relatively small preponderance of males over females. The English immigration to the Chesapeake had not been confined to a short period, but had been continuous, from 1607 on, with various peaks of intensity—in all, an immigrant population eight times as large as the Puritan migration. This century-long flow had consisted overwhelmingly of unmarried male indentured servants (males outnumbered females by well over six to one), bound in indentures to four or more years of servitude, depending largely on age, and traveling not in family groups but as individuals. They had arrived and had been put to work in an unfamiliar, unhealthy environment in which malaria, which opened its victims to the ravages of a dozen other diseases, was endemic, and they had died like flies.

A deadly cycle had been at work. Survival in this environment had depended on building up immunities to the worst diseases, and these immunities were strongest in those born in the land. But there was no quick development of a native-born population. The immigrant women, too few under the best of conditions to reproduce the local populations, were kept by servitude from early marriages, and they succumbed like the men to the diseases that swept the land. The children they bore, hence the native population, were too few to replace the losses, even if all their children had lived. In fact, approximately half of the children born in these disease-ridden colonies in the seventeenth century died before the age of twenty, and those who survived to that age—the most-seasoned and best-acclimatized people of the region—had a further life expectancy of little over twenty years; New Englanders aged twenty had almost twice that life expectancy. And these were the natives; most immigrants to the

Chesapeake who survived to the age of twenty died before reaching forty.

The deadly cycle of high death rates requiring more and more immigration to stock the work force, hence a constant renewal of the same disease vulnerability—this cycle could only be broken either by the slow growth of a native-born population, which would eventually have the advantages of a balanced sex ratio and inborn resistance to local diseases, or by the shift to a different source of manpower. Both were taking place in the years when our legates were touring the land. Slowly the proportion of native-born Virginians and Marylanders had grown. It was just at the time we are discussing—at the end of the seventeenth century—that the number of native-born whites finally became greater than that of white immigrants; it was then, and then only, that the white population was beginning to reproduce itself without immigration. At the same time the work force was in the midst of a dramatic shift to slave labor. As late as 1680 less than 8 percent of the Chesapeake population had been black slaves; by 1690 the figure was 15 percent; by 1710 it was 25 percent. And the percentage was continuing to rise, not because planters preferred blacks to whites, and not because they feared open revolt by a rural proletariat of freed white servants, but because the available sources of British indentured servants were disappearing. In the late seventeenth century the supply of indentured servants dropped by 3 percent a year while the demand for labor grew at about the same rate. To fill the growing gap in field labor the planters turned increasingly to slaves, whose availability soared after 1697, when the monopoly of the Royal African Company was broken and the African slave trade was thrown open to all comers.

As a result of this shift there was under way in 1700 —our legates would have observed—a massive transformation. A slave labor force that could be recruited at will by those with capital to invest was creating a growing disparity in the size of the producing units, and at the same time generating a self-intensifying tendency toward oligarchy. More and more of the productive land was devolving into the hands of a few large-scale operators, while more and more of the white population owned less and less of the best agricultural lands, were in a weak competitive situation, and were drifting into tenancy and moving off to more easily accessible frontier lands. At the same time a small number of ambitious landowning planters—a William Byrd I, a William Fitzhugh, a Wormeley, a Lee, a Carter, a Beverley—were able to parlay small gains into the critical capital of slaves, maneuver politically to get the lands they wanted, and begin the process of gentrification.[6]

Their achievements by 1700 were still modest by metropolitan standards. Byrd, a goldsmith's son who made his fortune by aggressive exploitation of the backcountry Indian trade, was able to send *his* son to England for his entire education and to support him in style as he learned commerce, law, and the ways of the polite world. But the senior Byrd's Westover plantation house was not the elegant riverside mansion it would later become; it was a four-square wooden farmhouse built for utility and with no pretense to elegance. The greatest house of the late seventeenth century was probably Greenspring, which had been Governor Berkeley's home and political head-quarters during his long tenure in office. The legates would have found that house in a significant state of transition. At the time of their visit the original manor house—"a typical small English brick country house" of the 1640s, which measured in all only sixty feet by sixty—was being renovated and rebuilt into a 2½-story mansion house a hundred feet long, boasting two tiers of dormers in its high-pitched roof, a five-arched arcade shading the lower front, and a second-floor porch with ornamental brickwork. Even so, a century later, just before the house was demolished, the noted architect Benjamin Latrobe inspected it and described it as "a brick building of great solidity but no attempt at grandeur"; its ornamented brickwork, he wrote, was "clumsy," and "about the style of James the first."[7]

There were, in 1700, other houses of some amplitude if no great technical elegance—Ralph Wormeley's Rosegill, the ten-room "great house" of a sprawling, multibuilding farm establishment built on a bluff overlooking the Rappahannock River; William Fitzhugh's Bedford, a thirteen-room wooden structure on the Potomac, four rooms of which were hung with tapestries and which was surrounded by the usual cluster of outbuildings, by an orchard of 2,500 apple trees, and by a large fenced-in garden. In Maryland too a nascent aristocracy was beginning to express its social ambitions and self-regard in the enhancement of the physical setting of its existence. But

these late seventeenth-century establishments, much remarked on at the time, were the merest winks of light in
a universe of frontier desolation. Virginia, a group of
residents reported in 1697, "looks all like a wild desart; the
high-lands overgrown with trees, and the low-lands sunk
with water, marsh, and swamp . . . perhaps not the hun-
dredth part of the country is yet clear'd from the woods,
and not one foot of the marsh and swamp drained."
Where the still heavily forested land was cleared, there
were tree stumps and tangles of shrubs in and around
small patches of cultivation.

The typical house of an ordinary farmer was a dark,
drafty, dirt-floored, insect-ridden, one- or two-bedroom
box made of green wood and scarcely worth maintaining
in good condition, since it would be abandoned as soon as
the few acres of farmland it adjoined were exhausted by
ruthless tobacco cultivation. These ill-kept, ramshackle,
crowded little farmhouses, so flimsy they were "virtually
uninhabitable after a decade unless they were substantially
reconstructed," were "dribbled over the landscape without apparent design." Most were a mile or so from the next
habitation (some were completely isolated), and there
were ruins and debris all along the banks of Chesapeake
Bay and the lower reaches of the rivers that empty into it,
wherever there was, or had been, habitation.[8]

Precisely what our legates would have seen in their
water-borne inspection tour of 1700 has been vividly, and
accurately, described by a modern scholar. Riding along
the Maryland rivers at that time, Gloria Main has written,
one would have seen

vast unbroken stands of gigantic trees along the spines of higher ground, interspersed by abandoned fields and overgrown thickets with occasional sagging houses and dilapidated barns. The long intervals of green shoreline are only occasionally interrupted by villagelike clusters of small buildings that mark the home plantations of the larger planters, but nowhere would we see great mansions rising from grassy knolls or long sweeps of lawn leading down to the waterside. The landings to which we tie up our boat lead us instead to small wooden houses, unpainted and unadorned. No formal space stands before or behind the principal structure, if one can so be defined, nor is there an orderly disposition of the farm buildings. Only the beaten pathways between link them together as a working whole.

If the untidy, unplanned, and unsymmetrical layout of the typical plantation is dismaying, the interiors of the homes prove even bleaker. There we find few comforts and no conveniences. Most colonial furniture consists of homemade pieces from local soft woods, roughly dressed and nailed together. Dirt or plank floors bear no coverings, nor do curtains hang at the glassless windows.

The commissioners would have found few concentrations of people, red, white, or black, anywhere. There were no towns, nor any general interest in creating them because the House of Burgesses, the report of 1697 stated, consisted largely of country people born in the land, people who had never seen a town and had no idea of their "conveniency."[9] Even small groups of people would have been found only in a few of the inland villages, which consisted of a courthouse, a church, and a market of some

kind. And the outer frontier was still close to the coast—
in the near piedmont region, just beyond the reach of
river navigation, between eighty and a hundred miles
distant from the sea. It was in that piedmont frontier, in
the years of this Domesday survey, that new lands were
being claimed and opened up, and it seemed a wilderness
world. When in 1714 Governor Spotswood settled Virginia's first German colony, a group of forty ironworkers
from Nassau-Siegen on the Rhine, in an encampment of
palisaded log cabins just inside the fringe of the piedmont
forests, he knew he was condemning them to a wilderness
existence. In fact this crude settlement, which he called
Germanna, was only thirty miles from the fall line and
equally close to well-settled territory to the north, along
the Potomac River.[10]

Touring deeper inland along the Virginia rivers, our
legates would have passed through a succession, not of
massive plantation estates and genteel establishments
manned by platoons of slaves, but of moderate-sized and
small farms, most of them worked by their owners with
one or two servants or slaves. Virginia's rent roll of 1704,
covering the area from the Rappahannock River south,
reveals approximately 5,500 separate units of landownership. While there were a few tracts of several thousand
acres (most of them only lightly cultivated frontier reserves), the great majority of these Virginia farms were
holdings of from fifty to five hundred acres, and the
mixed work force of servants and slaves (the slaves out-
numbering the servants by 20 percent) was distributed
thinly through these plantations. The average Virginia
farm had only one or two servants or slaves; "a bare

handful of well-to-do men each [had] from five to ten, or in rare cases 20 or 30, servants or slaves." And as they progressed still deeper inland, the main habitations the legates would have found would have been Indian cabins, "built," a contemporary wrote, "with posts put into the ground, the one by the other as close as they could stand . . . and a sort of roof upon it, covered with the bark of trees. They say it keeps out the rain very well. The Indian women were all naked, only a girdle they had tied around the waist and about a yard of blanketing put between their legs. . . . Their beds were mats made of bulrushes. . . . All the household goods was a pot."[11]

The only busy scenes anywhere would have been the dock areas at the mouth of the James and a few other spots along the Chesapeake Bay basin where the tobacco fleet, loaded with huge barrels of the weed that had been rolled to the river banks and carried downstream on rafts or skiffs, rode at anchor awaiting departure. There incoming vessels, arriving with loads of goods, servants, and slaves, carried news of an incomparably greater world far over the horizon.

But however crude and thinly populated the Chesapeake world was, it was active, more or less stable, and beginning to produce a culturally ambitious gentry leadership. In comparison with the settlements in the Carolinas—the fourth and last area of the legates' inspection—it was civilization itself.

There were two centers of British habitation south of Virginia which together would have formed the commissioners' fourth and final circuit. The older, which would become North Carolina, was only twenty to thirty miles south of Virginia. In 1700 this cluster of settlements around Albemarle Sound was a scraggly sprawl of farms and tiny villages set in the midst of pine forests and planted in the sandy soil of a coastal region cut off from the ocean by a ring of sand reefs. To this sheltered, almost inaccessible region had come as early as the 1650s a ragtag collection of farmers, trappers, petty merchants, Indian traders, and rather desperate fortune hunters. Most had come from, or via, Virginia, which at that time regarded this pine-forest wilderness as its southern frontier; later they were joined by groups of Marylanders, New Englanders, and Barbadians. By 1700 new and alien groups were beginning to arrive. In 1704–1705 a colony of Huguenots, escaping from crowded conditions in Virginia, joined the settlements. And in 1710 a colony of Swiss and Germans formed a separate settlement somewhat to the south, on the Neuse River. Some of these new settlers were religious radicals —Baptists, Anabaptists, and Mennonites—seeking refuge from a strict Protestant regime in Bern, Switzerland. But to this original group had been added several hundred of the ten thousand refugees from the southwest Rhineland who had arrived in England in 1710 and had then scattered into remote corners of the British world—some to Ireland, some to the Schoharie Valley of New York, some to the backcountry of Pennsylvania, some to the pine woods of North Carolina.

So the northern Carolina settlement of a few thousand

souls was being peopled—quite randomly—from several quite different sources. The inhabitants, living in rough, scruffy clearings at the edges of pine forests and in dwellings even cruder than those of the Chesapeake farmers, were engaged in tobacco-growing, mixed farming, and cattle-raising. They were few in number; they formed no towns of any size; and they nourished no gentry leadership. Their still primitive settlements were highly unstable, and the commissioners, as they left, must have wondered if they would survive at all. For the establishment of New Bern, North Carolina, had touched off an Indian war, which broke out in September 1711 and raged for two years. It would end, after orgies of atrocities on both sides, with the neighboring Tuscarora tribes decimated and driven off the land. That it was "won" at all—that is, that the northern Carolina settlements survived at all—was due in part to the help provided by the southern Carolina settlements. Several expeditions of southern Carolinians together with warlike Indian allies marched across the three hundred miles of unmapped forests that separated the two regions, through veritable jungles and scarcely passable swamp land, to help repel the Tuscaroras' attacks in the north.[12]

These southern Carolinians had come from a tiny but surprisingly prosperous community centered on the port of Charles Town, at the juncture of the Ashley and Cooper rivers. In 1703, in this southernmost British settlement there were just over 7,000 inhabitants (somewhat more than lived in the northern area). It was a population strangely proportioned: almost half were black slaves, Indians, or white indentured servants. The free whites—a mere 3,600—were the product of a straggling immigration, chiefly from Barbados. Desperately attempting to wring profits from the wild land, they were experimenting with raising silkworms, cotton, flax, and rice while developing forest industries and raising cattle. Their way of life, at the turn of the century, was primitive. Working in the semitropical climate side by side with their black and Indian slaves, they shared at times "a common undertaking as members of an interracial family unit," but it was a unit that was explosive with half-controlled tensions, fears, and hostilities. Miscegenation was commonplace; mulatto and "mustee" (mixed Negro and Indian) children were everywhere; and manumission was frequent—of mulatto children and of black and Indian women (not men). These were no tender, affectionate relationships. This was a brutal, half-primitive world of bushwhacking frontiersmen, who "can't be persuaded," the Anglican missionary Francis Le Jau, reported in 1709, "that Negroes and Indians are otherwise than beasts, and use them like such." So Mary Stafford, a young woman who, with her husband, had fled England for South Carolina to escape their debts, wrote in 1711 that there were good possibilities in the colony—for those who could "get a few slaves and can beat them well to make them work hard. [T]here is no living here without."[13]

It was in fact the South Carolinians' toughness, their crudeness, and their fierce Conquistador-like zest for profits that made possible their major source of gain. For the Indian trade was their Potosí, and it was an enterprise of ferocious, often bloody, exploitation. In the early 1700s there were at least 200 white traders working out of Charles Town. They organized caravans of 20 or 30 pack horses which they led or sent not merely 145 miles inland to a central Indian transfer point near present-day Columbia, South Carolina, but deep into southern Georgia to barter—with whatever ruthlessness was effective—with the Creek tribes, and all the way across Georgia, across Alabama, and across Mississippi, on treks that took a year or more, to reach the Chickasaw tribes on the Mississippi River. By 1700 an average of 54,000 deerskins were being exported annually to England from the still primitive settlements in southern Carolina—cargoes worth a small fortune. It was this Indian trade—with its half-savage British *coureurs de bois,* many of them accepted members of the Indian tribes in which they lived for most of each year; with its caravans coming and going; with its transfer centers and warehouses, its canoes and flat boats in which skins could be transported in large quantities along river routes—it was all of this strange and exotic traffic that would have struck the commissioners most forcefully as they completed the fourth circuit in Charles Town.[14]

This is what British North America must have looked like in 1700, this is what William III's commissioners would have had to report—not in the rigid formulas of the original Domesday Book, with its abbreviated listings of tenures and real property, but in a looser form, which would have described how the "land . . . was peopled and with what sort of men."

But there is a larger dimension to the story that the legates should have reported if they were faithful to their instructions.

These widely scattered settlements, for all their differences, shared a single, complex characteristic, a common quality, which was just then emerging and which would continue to characterize American society throughout the pre-industrial era and perhaps afterward as well. It forms my fourth proposition, which is as follows:

Proposition Four

American culture in this early period becomes most fully comprehensible when seen as the exotic far western periphery, a marchland, of the metropolitan European culture system.

This whole world of the legates' inspection was a borderland, a part of the expanding periphery of Britain's core culture; and its inner quality derived from that fact. Like the Welsh borderland two hundred years earlier, like the Scottish middle marches a century earlier, like Ireland and the Caribbean islands in the colonists' own time, and like Australia later, the mainland North American colonies formed a typically disordered border country in which, as in the Scottish marchland in the fifteenth century, "violence [was] . . . a way of life."[15] Concentrating, as American historians have done, on the origins of a later American civilization, and hence viewing the colo-

nial world as a *frontier*—that is, as an advance, as a for-
ward- and outward-looking, future-anticipating progress
toward what we know eventuated, instead of as a periphery, a ragged outer margin of a central world, a regressive,
backward-looking diminishment of metropolitan accom-
plishment—looking at the colonies in this anachronistic
way, one tends to minimize the primitiveness and violence, the bizarre, quite literally outlandish quality of life
in this far-distant outback of late seventeenth-century
Britain.

Partly this wildness, extravagance, and disorder were
simply the products of the inescapable difficulties of
maintaining a high European civilization in an undeveloped environment. Partly, too, they were products
of the hostility that developed between the Europeans
and the native peoples. But in large part, too, they were
products of the common European, and indeed British,
conception of America as an uncivil place on the distant
margins of civilization—a place where the ordinary re-
straints of civility could be abandoned in pell-mell exploitation, a remote place where recognized enemies and
pariahs of society—heretics, criminals, paupers—could
safely be deposited, their contamination sealed off by
three thousand miles of ocean, and where putatively in-
ferior specimens of humanity, blacks and Indians, could
be reduced to subhuman statuses, worked like animals,
and denied the most elemental benefits of law and religion, those fragile integuments which even in England
could barely contain the savagery of life. Blackstone's
statement in his *Commentaries* that "a slave or negro, the

instant he lands in England, becomes a freeman; that is, the law will protect him in the enjoyment of his person and his property," and Mansfield's decision in *Sommersett's Case* (1772), were simply obvious[16]; but obvious too was the obverse understanding that on the outer boundaries of civilization, restraint on brutal exploitation could be abandoned.

There was nothing remarkable in such a view. The peripheries generally were viewed like this. So land-rich Ireland and its brutally subjugated people were seen at the time (and, one might add, after); so too the sugar-rich West Indies; so too, later, Australia and New Zealand, and ultimately parts of Africa. What was uncommon, and what created the distinctive characteristics of British North American life, was the fact that by the turn of the seventeenth century the settlers in America—the Creole, now indigenous population—had attained a state of self-conscious gentility incompatible with the violence and extravagance and disorder of life in a marchland, and they were aware that that was so. It was the juxtaposition of the two—the intermingling of savagery and developing civilization—that is the central characteristic of the world that was emerging in British America. Borderland violence and bizarre distensions of normal European culture patterns had become fused with a growing civility into a distinctive way of life.

Everywhere one turns in this far periphery of the British world one finds examples of this complex mixture. The Indian wars are the most obvious. They bred a brutality so extreme that one almost tries not to comprehend.

Kindly, devout, and genteel householders became brutal overnight. The gentle, humane Reverend John Pike of Dover, New Hampshire, calmly recorded in his journal of 1682–1709 a fearful chronicle, not merely of sudden death and kidnapping, but of savagery, on both sides. William Moodey, Pike reported, was captured, then escaped, and was retaken: " 'tis feared he & another Englishman were roasted to death." Two of the white women captured by the Indians in the Haverhill raid of March 1697, he recorded—and Cotton Mather and others celebrated—managed to break free; and then these New England women "slew ten of the Indians, & returned home with their scalps." Pike might have added that among these slaughtered and scalped Indian victims of the two Haverhill women—the mother and nurse of an infant whose brains had been "dashed out . . . against a tree" by the Indians—were two native women and six children, and that the colony, following a policy common at the time, paid the Haverhill ladies £50 in bounty money for the scalps they brought back. And he might have noted further that scalping, indulged in by whites as well as by Indians everywhere in this period, was no deft tonsorial operation but a work of butchery in which, more often than not, the cranium was shattered with an axe; the victims were as often living as dead when it was done.[17]

The savagery of the Indian wars was the same everywhere. In the Tuscarora War in North Carolina, terrified white settlers, some newly arrived from Europe, burned Indians alive in retaliation for what had happened to their women: "laid on their house-floors and great stakes run

up through their bodies. Others big with child, the infants ripped out and hung upon trees." And so it continued. A half-century later one of the defenders of a besieged fort in South Carolina's Cherokee War (1760–1761) wrote the governor, "We have now the pleasure, Sir, to fatten our dogs with their carcasses and to display their scalps neatly ornamented on the top of our bastions." That fierce and bloody war, wrote the eighteenth-century historian David Ramsay, "tainted the principles of many of the inhabitants, so as to endanger the peace and happiness of society." Respectable backcountry people, he said, "acquired such vicious habits that when the war was over they despised labor and became pests of society," creating in the backcountry a constant state of "anarchy, disorder, and confusion."[18]

But the meaning of the Indian wars cannot be measured simply by events like this, nor was their effect confined to those directly involved. The narratives of Indian captivity—best sellers everywhere in America with the appearance of *The Soveraignty & Goodness of God . . . Being a Narrative of the Captivity and Restauration of Mrs. Mary Rowlandson . . .* (1682)—universalized these experiences, cast them into popular literary idioms, and drove them, in ways one will never fully understand, deep into the American psyche. Contemporary readers of those vivid tales, the more gripping because they told of fearful things that in fact happened to many hundreds of their contemporaries and that might happen to anyone in America,[19] must have incorporated the narrators' experiences into their basic perception of the world. They must

somehow have learned to live with the constant apprehension of extreme violence, and they must have wondered, secretly, guiltily, about their own capacity to endure—and to inflict—degradation, humiliation, and pain.[20]

But one need not dwell on the Indian wars, so full of atrocities on both sides, bred of fear and an insensitivity to human suffering. They seem too obvious an example and somehow not a part of the normal pattern of life. But savagery and the breakdown of ordered life lay everywhere in this borderland world, especially on its own margins. The North Carolina backwoodsmen were repeatedly said to be "the lowest scum and rabble . . . [who] build themselves sorry hutts and live in a beastly sort of plenty . . . devoted to calumny, lying, and the vilest tricking and cheating; a people into whose heads no human means can beat the notion of a publick interest or persuade to live like men." The South Carolina Indian traders were known to be "more prone to savage barbarity than the savages themselves." "Villains," "horse thieves," "banditti" infested the southern border country, it was said again and again. And travelers at the outposts at every stage—Esopus (Kingston), New York, in the mid-seventeenth century; New Bern, North Carolina, in 1710; Pittsburgh and the Ohio country in the 1760s and 1770s—reported hard-drinking trappers and traders mingling with pioneer farmers, scenes of drunken brawls involving whites, blacks, and Indians, at times an almost complete breakdown of normal civility.[21]

Savagery lay not only on the far outer margins, however. In the south, and elsewhere as well, it invaded the very heart of a growing gentility. For in those colonies slavery took on a new and strange existence. In British North America slavery was no exterior and distant phenomenon, sealed off in remote regions as it was for Britain itself, but, in its most brutal form, an everyday fact of life in communities that were otherwise genteel, otherwise decent, and growing more tolerant, reasonable, and benign all the time. In plantation culture, and elsewhere where slavery was an important part of society, an accommodation was somehow made between brutality and progressive refinement. The savagery of chattel slavery was no new thing for people of the seventeenth and eighteenth centuries; brutality in human relations was commonplace, and took many forms. What was new was that chattel slavery, a condition considered appropriate for isolated work gangs at the remote margins of civilization, was here incorporated into a world of growing sophistication.

One can hardly believe William Byrd II's normal way of life, as he so meticulously recorded it in the diary he kept during these years at the turn of the century. The days pass smoothly. Byrd rises "betimes," reads his Bible, a passage in Greek, another in Hebrew, and some poetry, does a few exercises, and attends to the duties of his plantation, Westover, which he was building into the elegant Georgian estate that would become so famous. But in the midst of all this gentility lie his relations with his slaves. His black serving girl Jenny, age sixteen, is beaten repeatedly. Scarcely a month goes by in which she is not thrashed, beaten, soundly whipped (his terms) for all sorts of things, for something and for nothing: for being unmannerly, for concealing the serving boy Eugene's bedwetting, for throwing water on the sofa. She is strapped, beaten with tongs, and on one occasion, when Byrd's neurotic wife flies into a rage, branded with a hot iron. And the eighteen-year-old Eugene is whipped soundly for running away (Byrd could not imagine why he would want to do such a thing), then clamped with the iron boot; thereafter, when his bedwetting becomes chronic and when even the branding iron does no good, "I made him drink a pint of piss."[22]

Yet Byrd was a well-educated and conscientious *paterfamilias,* a would-be *littérateur,* proud of his large, much-used library; he was a man of taste and cultivation who had lived for fifteen years among the literati of London and had studied at the Inns of Court. His treatment of his slaves was by no means exceptionally brutal. For exceptional behavior one need merely turn over the letters of the South Carolina missionary Le Jau, with their tales of slave women being "scalloped" and left to die in the woods or burnt alive on suspicion of arson; of masters who "hamstring, mai[m], & unlimb" their slaves "for small faults," or for falling asleep at work "scourge" them twice a day, then "muffle" them so that they could not eat, and at night bind them into a "hellish machine . . . [in] the shape of a coffin where [they] could not stirr"; of laws, no longer even remarked on, that required the castration of Negro runaways; and of Indian wars deliberately instigated "for our people to get slaves." Byrd was more typical than these South Carolina masters, and typical too must have been the psychological conflicts that produced the rages of the politically liberal, well-read, and responsible Landon Carter. Carter's diary—as I read it—is a tragic and despairing document, and it could have been written nowhere else in the Western world—except, perhaps, in the remote far *Eastern* marchland of European civilization, on the isolated estates of the Russian nobility, whose autonomy was as complete as that of the American plantation owners and who also sought to incorporate a total despotism into the heart of domestic gentility.[23]

Still, slavery, like the Indian wars, may somehow be discounted as being exceptional to most people's way of life (in fact it was not) or as a commonplace of the age. But slavery, like the Indian wars, was only a particular expression of a mingling of primitivism and progressive civilization which in its widest ranges was an underlying characteristic of all these marchland colonies. It was thus perfectly reasonable for the British government to think of the American colonies as in some sense frontier garrison settlements, and to appoint military officers to rule them, which they did throughout the seventeenth century and for the first third of the eighteenth century. It was equally reasonable for the government to start the practice, which it did in the early seventeenth century, of banishing convicted felons or prisoners of war to the colonies: "so do the Spaniards people the Indies," Governor Dale of Virginia wrote in 1611 in begging the government to send over to the labor-short colony "all offenders out of the common gaols condemned to die." In the course of the eighteenth century Britain would send over to North America, mainly to Maryland and Virginia, an estimated fifty thousand convicted felons, approximately the same number of convicts that would be sent to Australia before 1824. Indeed, garrison government and the transport of convicts to America were aspects of the same core-and-periphery relationship. As a form of punishment, transportation was logical enough, for the colonies were assumed to be so remote, so primitive, that merely sending people there would be punitive, and it was also economical, constructive, and socially therapeutic—for Britain, that is: the colonies were seen as different kinds of places.[24]

The colonists, however, were beginning to disagree. As early as 1670 the Virginia Assembly attempted to ban the transportation of "fellons and other desperate villaines sent hither from the several prisons in England." They feared, they said, "the danger which apparently threatens us from the barbarous designes and felonious practices of such wicked villaines." More than that, the Assembly wrote, by importing convicted criminals we "loose our reputation, [whilst] we are beleived to be a place onely fitt to receive such base and lewd persons"—or, as President Stith of the College of William and Mary put it later, in the eighteenth century, Virginia, because of the advent of the convicts, had come to be reputed a "hell upon earth, another Siberia." One well-informed commentator in early eighteenth-century Virginia felt that the only solution, since the government was determined to continue shipping criminals to America, was to set off one whole county in Virginia as a separate penal colony—an American Botany Bay, in effect—and confine all the transported felons to that area. By then, 1724, the incongruity and illogicality of shipping convicted felons to the colonies were disturbing; thirty years later the practice had become shocking. Dismissal of the "terrible herd of exiled malefactors" to the mainland colonies, proud of their gentility, it was then said, was a punishment not to the convicts, for whom it was in fact a blessing, but for the Americans, who had done no wrong. Americans were Britons: "how injurious does it seem to free one part of the dominions from the plagues of mankind, and cast them upon another?" By the 1760s the situation, to many Americans, had become ludicrous, a fit subject for Franklin's choicest wit.[25]

All of these overt violations of ordinary civil order—Indian wars, slavery, garrison government, the transportation of criminals—though they permeated the developing culture, overspecify and overdramatize, make too lurid, an issue that had much subtler and broader manifestations. The less physical aspects of the colonies' peculiarities were equally important. For ultimately the colonies' strange ways were only distensions and combinations of elements that existed in the parent cultures, but that existed there within constraints that limited, shaped, and in a sense civilized their growth. These elements were here released, fulfilled—at times with strange results that could not have been anticipated.

Thus Puritanism, in its various forms, fulfilled itself in New England, reached its limits, unconstrained by a parent church or by any external social or institutional authority. It became complex and engrossing in its unfolding; bred unusual offshoots; and ended by creating a peculiar subculture of its own.[26] So too, late in the century, did the products of a wave of pietistic fervor that broke over the German states. Everywhere in the Rhineland this pietistic awakening created new radical movements, but they were movements whose European shapes were formed and whose European destinies were limited by the establishments in whose interstices alone these movements were able to grow. In the far western American marchlands, where there were no external controls, no central establishment, the results were altogether different.

It was in Pennsylvania that the messianic pietism and the bizarre occultism that swept through the Protestant sects in the German states—perfectionist impulses that tended to exhaust themselves in the dense social environment of Europe—it was in Pennsylvania that they bore the strangest and most plentiful fruit.[27]

It began with the arrival in 1694 of the learned Johannes Kelpius and his mystical sect, until then known as the Chapter of Perfection. Kelpius was a model Rosicrucian mystic, a magus, and also a *magister* of the University of Altdorf, a master both of esoteric lore and of secular scholarship. With his followers, he built just outside Philadelphia, on a ridge overlooking a creek, a logwalled monastery forty feet by forty feet to accommodate the forty brethren. It had a common room for Quakerlike worship, and individual cells where the brethren could search for perfection in trancelike states by contemplating their magic numbers and their esoteric symbols. In a primitive laboratory they conducted chemical and pharmaceutical experiments aimed at eliminating disease and prolonging life indefinitely. And on the roof they built a telescope, which they manned from dusk till dawn, so that in case, as they put it, the Bridegroom came in the middle of the night, their lamps would be prepared— which is to say, they would be prepared to receive the Deliverer. But the heart of Kelpius's sect—which was renamed here The Woman in the Wilderness, after a passage in Revelation—lay not in the common room, not in the cells, not in the laboratory, and not in the rooftop *Sternwarte*, but in a cave which the Magus found in a nearby hillside and in which he spent most of his life after his arrival in Pennsylvania pondering a truth concealed to ordinary souls but revealed to him by signs, by symbols, by numbers, and by pure contemplation. For he knew with certainty that the wilderness into which the Woman in Revelation (the pure church) had fled was none other than Pennsylvania. It was here, he believed, that mankind would "find the dear Lord Jesus"; it was here that the true Christian, vigilantly trimming his lamp, should await the Bridegroom and prepare for the heavenly feast.[28]

At Kelpius's death the leadership of The Woman in the Wilderness passed to Johann Gottfried Seelig, a theologian and scholar of such immaculate piety and stern austerity that he could not tolerate the worldly demands even of guiding a monastery, and so resigned, "clad himself in pilgrim garb, and retired to one of the small log cabins that were on the tract, where he spent his time in mystical speculations and devout meditations, in which the spiritual bridegroom bore an important part." His successor, Conrad Matthäi, was the last in this succession; he lived until 1748. *Der alte Matthäi,* as he was called, became a familiar figure to everyone in and around Philadelphia, impressive to the end with his snow-white hair and flowing beard, dressed in a coarse homespun gown and sandals, and carrying always a long staff, an alpenstock, which must have seemed a symbol of office.[29]

But long before the sect's and Matthäi's demise, the brotherhood of The Woman in the Wilderness had been superseded in the Pennsylvania mystics' world by a far more dynamic movement led by the most extraordinary figure of them all.

Johann Conrad Beissel, an ignorant, mystical, tormented baker's boy from the German Palatinate, after flirting with several of the radical sects that struggled for existence in the spiritually burnt-over districts of the Rhineland, had joined the exodus to Pennsylvania; concocted, in a hermit's cabin near Germantown, his own brand of sabbatarian Dunkerism; gathered a band of followers at Conestoga; and founded the Ephrata cloister, whose monks and nuns he ruled despotically, neurotically, and cruelly. God-possessed, immersed in the writings of the mystics, entranced by the secret rites of the Rosicrucians, he was a cyclone of energy, and he pursued his dream of a pure religion, unimpeded by state, society, or church. He was bizarre but unconfined, and the fame of his strange sect of emaciated celibates spread throughout the English as well as the German population of Pennsylvania and ultimately throughout the Rhineland and in France, through Voltaire, as well. Beissel preached with his eyes shut tight, passionately, ungrammatically, in incoherent torrents. If by chance his bowed congregation indicated understanding in quiet murmurs of assent, he reversed his chaotic argument to demonstrate the incomprehensibility of God's truth. And he imposed on his half-starved followers—clothed in rough, Capuchin-like habits designed to hide all signs of human shape—a rule of such severe self-mortification that some went mad, while the elite enacted the secret rites of the Rosicrucians, to which neophytes sought admission by bodily ordeals that lasted forty days and forty nights. Yet . . . and yet . . . the art of book illumination was reinvented in Beissel's Ephrata, and from some spark of hidden genius the *Vorsteher* himself devised a form of polyphonic choral music, complete with his own system of notation, which, when sung falsetto by his followers straining to reach ever higher, more "divine" notes, created an unearthly effect that enthralled everyone who ever heard it—and which caught the imagination, two centuries later, of another German immigrant in America, Thomas Mann, who, brooding on art and the German soul, immortalized Beissel in *Doctor Faustus.* [30]

Beissel's Ephrata was unique—but such unique utopias grew like mushrooms in British North America, flourished, and then wilted and died in that open world. While contemplating a form for a Brotherhood of Zion fit for his prophetic ecstasies, Beissel visited first The

Woman in the Wilderness sect; then the Labadists' Bohemia Manor in nearby Maryland; and then the followers of Matthias Baumann, who believed they were as much Christ as Christ and could not sin and whose leader, to prove that he was a special envoy of God to man, proposed to walk across the surface of the Delaware River. And Beissel could have found many more. The sophisticated Moravian leader Count Zinzendorf considered Beissel to be diabolical, but Zinzendorf's own group, the Unitas Fratrum, contributed to the multiplicity of conventicles in America not only an array of semi-communistic Moravian settlements, but also a missionary movement that spawned dozens of short-lived utopias on the frontier and deep in Indian territory. The sectarian Germans—the so-called "plain Dutch"—who settled much of eastern Pennsylvania shared with Ephrata its alienation from the world and its relentless pursuit of truth; but having compromised to some extent with the world, they flourished. By 1750 there were forty-eight Amish and Mennonite settlements in Pennsylvania, ten Dunkard, and the beginnings of several Schwenkfelder.[31]

Much of the British North American culture was familiarly European, traditional, even conservative. Life on the farms outside Philadelphia, Francis Michel reported with surprise in 1704, was "just like living in Germany." But everywhere there were strange distensions of familiar forms, and an outer boundary of primitivism that entered into the inner lives of a population growing ever more genteel, ever more stable and sophisticated. And so it continued into the later eighteenth century. Sir William Johnson's establishment, Johnson Hall, the spacious, well-furnished mansion he built at the edge of the forest in the early 1760s just north of the Mohawk River in upcountry New York, was called by contemporaries a "superb and elegant edifice." But Johnson Hall was the headquarters building of a biracial manor court where Johnson lived the uninhibited life of a marchland baron, surrounded by his illegitimate children by two successive common-law wives, one a runaway German indentured servant, the other a Mohawk Indian, and by children of other, more casual connections as well. Crowds of Indians were always there. Outbuildings were constructed to accommodate them when they arrived, but many simply camped on the lawn and wandered through the house. Lord Adam Gordon, visiting in 1765, was astonished and deeply impressed by this strange baronial court "cleared," he reported, "in an absolute forest." Johnson's success with the Indians, he felt, and his control of this northern border area, were admirable, but, Gordon added after spending some days with Johnson, "no consideration should tempt me to lead his life. . . . I know no other man equal to so disagreeable a duty."[32]

Johnson's bizarre establishment was at the far edge of the outer periphery, but every section of the land, no matter how long settled and sophisticated, had direct and continuous contact with the wilderness. Mule skinners plunged deep into strange Indian territories, remained there for months, even years, to return to the coastal towns with packs of animal skins and with strange tales and stranger experiences they could never fully tell. Hundreds of settlers, we do not know how many, who made direct contact with the Indian tribes—even some of those captured and brutalized by the Indians during the wars—found in the Indians' lives an appealing sense of community, of equality, and of unfettered freedom of movement, and they disappeared across the forest pale. All the borderlands bred strange forms of life. William Faulkner's story of the mysterious Thomas Sutpen—erecting in frontier Mississippi, with the labor of twenty "wild" Negroes clothed only in caked mud, a mansion house made of bricks baked on the spot, which he equipped with costly European furnishings—has dramatic counterparts in the pages of history. So William Dunbar, a young Anglo-Scottish intellectual and scientist, constructed, in 1773, with the labor of a battalion of slaves he personally led in chains from Jamaica, a sumptuous wilderness estate at a deserted bend of the Mississippi River near Natchez. Dunbar's life, recorded in a diary that details his scientific studies as well as his struggle with his slaves and with the wilderness, is in some ways stranger and darker than that of any of Faulkner's characters. But the most extraordinary Faulknerian episode took place not on the banks of the Mississippi but in East Florida.[33]

Among the many whose imaginations were fired by the acquisition of East Florida in 1763 was a certain Dr. Andrew Turnbull of London, well connected with the leading politicians, including George Grenville, and with polite society. Like so many others he dreamed of founding an estate in that semitropical land that would produce cotton, silk, indigo, and fruits of all kinds; he also hoped it would provide comfort and affluence for his large and rather burdensome family. Being sophisticated, even scientific in his approach, he recruited settlers for his Florida land grant in places he believed had climates equivalent to Florida's, and so in 1768 arrived at the swampy Mosquito Inlet, 75 miles south of St. Augustine, with 1,255 Greeks, Corsicans, Italians, and Minorcans. The Greeks he had recruited in the villages of Mani in the Peloponnesus—villages "built like eagles' nests high on the cliffs of a rocky peninsula."

The saga of Turnbull's settlement, which he called New Smyrna, makes the bizarre early history of Faulkner's Yoknapatawpha County seem tranquil in comparison. The settlers, having deserted their dry, clear, invigorating Aegean and Mediterranean climate for Turnbull's swampy utopia, fell victim to Florida's heat, humidity, and torrential rains. Weakened by semi-starvation and malaria, they died in a rampage of disease. Within twenty-four months half of the settlers were dead, and Turnbull, his dream fading before his eyes, turned savage. Enforcing a criminal code of his own devising, he beat the survivors if they slackened in their work, and appointed sadistic overseers who turned the marshy, floridly overgrown plantation into a concentration camp. Those who attempted to flee were flogged, starved, and chained to heavy iron balls. Yet nothing could create the elysium Dr. Turnbull continued to seek. When the American Revolution loosened the ties of all civil authority in America, the surviving settlers finally managed to escape. Turnbull himself, pursued by creditors and enemies in high places in Florida, worked his way to Charleston, and there he lived out his life, a British subject to the end, a respected and successful physician, a man of property and standing, and one of the founders of the South Carolina Medical Society. His beautiful Greek wife, the last legacy of his earlier, bloody adventure, survived him.[34]

This mingling of primitivism and civilization, however transitory stage by stage, was an essential part of early American culture, and we must struggle to comprehend it.

What did it mean to Jefferson, slave owner and *philosophe*, that he grew up in this far western borderland world of Britain, looking out from Queen Anne rooms of spare elegance onto a wild, uncultivated land? We can only grope to understand.

Notes

Index

Notes

I

Worlds in Motion

1 Quoted in A. L. Rowse, "Tudor Expansion: The Transition from Medieval to Modern History," *William and Mary Quarterly*, 3rd ser., 14 (1957), 312. (This periodical will be cited hereafter as *W.M.Q.*) For a survey of domestic expansion and colonization in continental Europe, from classical antiquity to the fourteenth century, see Richard Koebner, "The Settlement and Colonization of Europe," in *The Cambridge Economic History of Europe*, I, ed. M. M. Postan (2nd ed., Cambridge, Eng., 1966), 1–91. Other essays in the same volume give details on colonization and expansion in specific countries and regions. There is no similar survey of domestic European colonization during and after the fourteenth century, but Karl F. Helleiner's essay "The Population of Europe from the Black Death to the Eve of the Vital Revolution" in vol. IV of the same series touches the subject at various points; see also C. T. Smith, *An Historical Geography of Western Europe before 1800* (New York, 1967), chap. 3. On early English expansion, see Maurice Beresford, *New Towns of the Middle Ages* (London, 1967). For an effort to conceptualize "British history" in global terms, as an "expanding zone of cultural conflict and creation," one of several such generative global population movements, see J. G. A. Pocock, "British History: A Plea for a New Subject," *Journal of Modern History*, 47 (1975), 601–621. For a different view of British expansionism, based on a systematic interpretation of the relations between "core" and "periphery" (illustrated chiefly by England and the Celtic fringe),

see Michael Hechter, *Internal Colonialism: The Celtic Fringe in British National Development, 1536–1966* (Berkeley and London, 1975). An exchange of views between Pocock and Hechter over these two quite different but equally imaginative projections follows Pocock's article, pp. 625–628. Cf. Pocock, "The Limits and Divisions of British History: In Search of the Unknown Subject," *American Historical Review,* 87 (April 1982), 311–336. (Hereafter, *A.H.R.*)

2 For a discussion of the recent proliferation of writing on early American history in a larger context, see Bernard Bailyn, "The Challenge of Modern Historiography," *ibid.,* 87 (Feb. 1982), 1–24.

3 Carville V. Earle, *The Evolution of a Tidewater Settlement System: All Hallow's Parish, Maryland, 1650–1783* (Univ. of Chicago, Dept. of Geography, Research Paper No. 170, 1975); Earle, "The First English Towns of North America," *Geographical Review,* 67 (1977), 34–50; Earle and Ronald Hoffman, "Staple Crops and Urban Development in the Eighteenth-Century South," *Perspectives in American History,* 10 (1976), 7–78; Earle and Hoffman, "The Urban South: The First Two Centuries," in *The City in Southern History,* eds. Blaine A. Brownell and David R. Goldfield (Port Washington, N.Y., 1977), chap. 2; Earle, "Environment, Disease, and Mortality in Early Virginia," in *The Chesapeake in the Seventeenth Century,* eds. Thad W. Tate and David Ammerman (New York, 1979), chap. 3; R. Cole Harris, "The Simplification of Europe Overseas," *Annals of the Association of American Geographers,* 67 (1977), 469–483; Harris, "European Beginnings in the Northwest Atlantic: A Comparative View," in *Seventeenth-Century New England,* eds. David D. Hall and David G. Allen (Boston, 1984), pp. 119–152; James T. Lemon, *The Best Poor Man's Country* (Baltimore, 1972); Lemon, "Early Americans and Their Social Environment," *Journal of Historical Geography,* 6 (1980), 115–131; D. W. Meinig, "The Continuous Shaping of America: A Prospectus for Geographers and Historians," *A.H.R.,* 83 (Dec. 1978), 1186–1205; Meinig, "American Wests: Preface to a Geographical Interpretation," *Annals of the Association of American Geographers,* 62 (1972), 159–184; H. Roy Merrens, *Colonial North Carolina in the Eighteenth Century* (Chapel Hill, N.C.,

1964); Merrens, "Historical Geography and Early American History," *W.M.Q.*, 22 (1965), 529–548; Joseph A. Ernst and Merrens, "Praxis and Theory in the Writing of American Historical Geography," *Journal of Historical Geography*, 4 (1978), 277–290; Robert D. Mitchell, *Commercialism and Frontier: Perspectives on the Early Shenandoah Valley* (Charlottesville, Va., 1977); Mitchell, "American Origins and Regional Institutions: The Seventeenth-century Chesapeake," *Annals of the Association of American Geographers*, 73 (1983), 404–420; Mitchell, "The Formation of Early American Cultural Regions: An Interpretation," in *European Settlement and Development in North America*, ed. James R. Gibson (Toronto, 1978), pp. 66–90. See also Douglas R. McManis, *Colonial New England: A Historical Geography* (New York, 1975). McManis's *Historical Geography of the United States: A Bibliography* (Ypsilanti, Mich., 1965), is a full and detailed listing, though many of the most suggestive works for the peopling theme have been published since this bibliography appeared.

4 The information in this and the following paragraphs summarizes sections of my *Voyagers to the West* (New York, 1986), which presents the full documentation.

5 Lowell C. Bennion, "Flight from the Reich: A Geographic Exposition of Southwest German Emigration, 1683–1815" (Ph.D. diss., Syracuse Univ., 1971), chaps. 1–3.

6 John J. McCusker and Russell R. Menard, *The Economy of British America, 1607–1789* (Chapel Hill, N.C., 1985), chap. 3.

7 Merrens, *Colonial North Carolina*, pp. 53, 54; A. Roger Ekirch, *"Poor Carolina": Politics and Society in Colonial North Carolina, 1729–1776* (Chapel Hill, N.C., 1981), esp. chap. 5 and map VIII; Harold E. Davis, *The Fledgling Province . . . Georgia, 1733–1776* (Chapel Hill, N.C., 1976), chap. 1, p. 14.

8 Terry L. Anderson and Robert P. Thomas, "White Population . . . the New England Economy in the Seventeenth Century," *Journal of Economic History*, 33 (1973), 634 ff. Averages of town settlements are worked out in a paper and accompanying maps by Lee Shai Weissbach, Harvard Univ., 1977. On the New Hampshire towns, John F. Looney, "Benning Wentworth's Land Grant Pol-

icy: A Reappraisal," *Historical New Hampshire,* 23 (1968), 3–13; Matt
B. Jones, *Vermont in the Making, 1750–1777* (Cambridge, Mass., 1939),
esp. appendix on Wentworth's town grants; Jere R. Daniell, *Experiment in Republicanism, New Hampshire . . . 1741–1794* (Cambridge,
Mass., 1970), pp. 15–16.

9 See especially, in addition to the publications cited in note 3 above,
Peter O. Wacker, *Land and People: A Cultural Geography of Pre-industrial New Jersey, Origins and Settlement Patterns* (New Brunswick, N.J., 1975).

10 Virginia D. Anderson, "To Pass beyond the Seas: The Great Migration and the Settlement of New England, 1630–1670" (Ph.D.
diss., Harvard Univ., 1984).

11 David W. Galenson, *White Servitude in Colonial America, an Economic Analysis* (Cambridge, Eng., 1981); Abbot E. Smith, *Colonists in Bondage* (Chapel Hill, N.C., 1947).

12 Mildred Campbell, "English Emigration on the Eve of the American Revolution," *A.H.R.,* 61 (Oct. 1955), 1–20, and "Social Origins of Some Early Americans," in *Seventeenth-Century America . . .,* ed.
James M. Smith (Chapel Hill, N.C., 1959); McCusker and Menard,
Economy of British America, pp. 242–243.

13 As noted below, there are very few detailed and suggestive writings
on the history of slaves in British North America, as distinct from
the history of views of slavery and of the Negro race. The most
informative are Peter H. Wood, *Black Majority: Negroes in Colonial
South Carolina, from 1670 through the Stono Rebellion* (New York,
1974); three essays by Allan L. Kulikoff: "The Origins of Afro-America Society in Tidewater Maryland and Virginia, 1700–1790,"
W.M.Q., 35 (1978), 226–259, "A 'Prolifick' People: Black Population
Growth in the Chesapeake Colonies, 1700–1790," *Southern Studies,*
16 (1977), 391–428, and "The Beginnings of the Afro-American Family in Maryland," in *Law, Society, and Politics in Early Maryland,*
eds. Aubrey C. Land *et al.* (Baltimore, 1977); and Philip D. Morgan,
"Black Life in Eighteenth-Century Charleston," *Perspectives in
American History,* new ser., 1 (1984), 187–232. The forthcoming
books by Kulikoff and Morgan on slaves and their society in early
America will advance the subject greatly. Of the extensive litera-

ture on the slave trade, see esp. Philip D. Curtin, *The Atlantic Slave Trade: A Census* (Madison, Wis., 1969); Henry A. Gemery and Jan S. Hogendorn, eds., *The Uncommon Market: Essays in the Economic History of the Atlantic Slave Trade* (New York, 1979); and Herbert S. Klein, *The Middle Passage* (Princeton, N.J., 1978), chap. 6.

14 The writings on the New England communities, which have still not been adequately summarized or interpreted, now include the work of David G. Allen, Linda Auwers (Bissell), Christopher Collier, Edward M. Cook, Jr., Bruce Daniels, John Demos, Charles Grant, Philip J. Greven, Jr., Kenneth Lockridge, Gloria L. Main, Jackson Turner Main, John F. Martin, Susan L. Norton, Sumner C. Powell, Darrett B. Rutman, Daniel Scott Smith, John J. Waters, William Willingham, and Michael Zuckerman. For an estimation of four of the most important studies of New England communities, see Jack P. Greene, "Autonomy and Stability . . .," *Journal of Social History*, 7 (1974), 171–194. The most recent such study, and one of the most provocative and most difficult to assimilate with the others, is Stephen Innes, *Labor in a New Land: Economy and Society in Seventeenth Century Springfield* (Princeton, N.J., 1983).

On Virginia and Maryland, see Wesley F. Craven, *White, Red, and Black: The Seventeenth-Century Virginian* (Charlottesville, 1971); and Edmund S. Morgan, *American Slavery, American Freedom* (New York, 1975), bk. II and appendix. The St. Mary's City Commission, working in the excellent Maryland Archives and the associated local collections, has concentrated on key problems, shown great ingenuity in analysis, and produced striking results. The most prolific author of the group is Russell R. Menard; his writings and those of others in this group are sampled and cited in *Law, Society, and Politics*, eds. Land *et al.*, and in *The Chesapeake in the Seventeenth Century*, eds. Tate and Ammerman, and summarized at various points in McCusker and Menard, *Economy of British America*. See also Paul G. Clemens, *The Atlantic Economy and Colonial Maryland's Eastern Shore* (Ithaca, N.Y., 1980). Two major books cap the work of these historians of the upper south: Gloria Main's *Tobacco Colony: Life in Early Maryland, 1650–1720* (Princeton, N.J., 1982), which incorporates most of the earlier findings and provides a vivid and harshly realistic picture of life in that desolate, exploitative outpost, from which only very gradually a civil and more or less genteel society was emerging, and Darrett B. Rutman and Anita H. Rutman, *A Place in Time: Middlesex County, Virginia, 1650–1750* (New York, 1984), an imaginative reconstruction of the life of one county in seventeenth-century Virginia, based on a computer-assisted assembling of biographical data pertaining to over 12,000 individuals who lived in the county between 1650 and 1750.

15 On the black population, see above, note 13, and in addition, Morgan, *American Slavery, American Freedom.* On the Indian population there are two comprehensive works: Bruce G. Trigger, ed., *Handbook of North American Indians,* XV *(Northeast)* (Washington, D.C., 1978), which contains nineteen descriptive essays on the east coastal Indian tribes, and James L. Axtell, *The European and the Indian: Essays in the Ethnohistory of Colonial North America* (New York, 1981), which concentrates on culture contacts, as does Neal Salisbury, *Manitou and Providence: Indians, Europeans, and the Making of New England, 1500–1643* (New York, 1982). There is in addition a variety of useful writings by Alden Vaughan and Wilcomb Washburn; a boiling polemic by Francis Jennings: *The Invasion of America* (Chapel Hill, N.C., 1975), which seeks to stand everything assumed to be true about the subject on its head; and Stephen Webb's *1676: The End of American Independence* (New York, 1984), bk. III, on the politics and diplomacy of the Iroquois tribes, a subject that has a considerable literature but that Webb freshly reconsiders. But a narrative history of the coastal North American Indian population is still almost impossible to assemble. Even the approximate size of the native population is in question. Only very recently, for example, has there been a systematic effort to correct the old and entirely misleading estimates of the size of the New England native population made originally by James Mooney and updated by A. L. Kroeber: see Sherburne F. Cook, *The Indian Population of New England in the Seventeenth Century* (Berkeley, 1976), and Salisbury, *Manitou and Providence,* pp. 22–30. For a recent bibliography by Axtell of early American ethnohistory, see

W.M.Q., 35 (1978), 110–144. Younger writers, notably James Merrell and Daniel Richter, whose work is just beginning to appear, are likely to deepen the subject considerably in the coming years.

16 E. E. Rich, "The Population of Elizabethan England," *Economic History Review*, 2d ser., 2 (1950), 247–265.

17 Alan Everitt, "Social Mobility in Early Modern England," *Past & Present*, 33 (1966), 56–73; Everitt, "Farm Labourers," in *The Agrarian History of England and Wales, IV (1500–1640)*, Joan Thirsk, ed. (Cambridge, Eng., 1967), chap. 7; John H. C. Patten, "Patterns of Migration and Movement of Labour to Three Pre-industrial East Anglian Towns," *Journal of Historical Geography*, 2 (1976), 111–129; Patten, *Rural-Urban Migration in Pre-industrial England* (Oxford Univ., School of Geography, *Research Papers* No. 6, 1973); Patten, "Population Distribution in Norfolk and Suffolk during the Sixteenth and Seventeenth Centuries," *Transactions of the Institute of British Geographers*, 65 (1975), 45–65; the essays by Penelope Corfield and Peter Clark, in *Crisis and Order in English Towns 1500–1700*, eds. Peter Clark and Paul Slack (London, 1972); P. J. Corfield, *The Impact of English Towns, 1700–1800* (Oxford, 1982), esp. pp. 102–107; Peter Clark, "Migration in England during the Late Seventeenth and Early Eighteenth Centuries," *Past & Present*, 83 (1979), 81–90, and his and David Souden's contributions to Peter Clark, ed., *The Transformation of English Provincial Towns, 1600–1800* (London, 1984). See also Wolfram Fischer, "Rural Industrialization and Population Change," *Comparative Studies in Society and History*, 15 (1973), 158–170. The work of the Cambridge Group to 1972 is summarized in the Introduction to Peter Laslett, ed., *Household and Family in Past Time* (Cambridge, Eng., 1972).

18 On the circulation of children in service, see Alan Macfarlane, *The Family Life of Ralph Josselin . . .* (Cambridge, Eng., 1970), pp. 205–210; Roger S. Schofield, "Age-Specific Mobility in an Eighteenth Century Rural English Parish," *Annales de Démographie Historique* (1970), 261–274; Peter Spufford, "Population Mobility in Pre-industrial England," *Genealogists' Magazine*, 17 (1973–1974), 420–429, 475–480, 537–543; Julian Cornwall, "Evidence of Popula-

tion Mobility in the Seventeenth Century," *Bulletin of the Institute of Historical Research*, 40 (1967), 150.

19 Patten, *Rural-Urban Migration*, p. 23; Lawrence Stone, "Social Mobility in England, 1500–1700," *Past & Present*, 33 (1966), 30–31; E. A. Wrigley, "A Simple Model of London's Importance in Changing English Society and Economy, 1650–1760," *ibid.*, 37 (1967), 44; Andrew B. Appleby, "Nutrition and Disease: The Case of London, 1550–1750," *Journal of Interdisciplinary History*, 6 (1975), 1–22 (for mortality tables see appendix, pp. 20–22).

20 Patten, *Rural-Urban Migration*, p. 27; Wrigley, "A Simple Model," pp. 46–47, 49–50.

21 R. J. Dickson, *Ulster Emigration to Colonial America, 1718–1775* (1966; rpt., Antrim, 1976), p. 3; M. Perceval-Maxwell, *The Scottish Migration to Ulster in the Reign of James I* (London, 1973), p. 313; L. M. Cullen, "Population Trends in Seventeenth-Century Ireland," *Economic and Social Review*, 6 (1975), 152–153.

22 Carl Bridenbaugh, *Vexed and Troubled Englishmen, 1590–1642* (New York, 1968), p. 434.

23 Rich, "Population of Elizabethan England," p. 263; David H. Sacks, *Trade, Society, and Politics in Bristol, 1500–1640* (New York, 1985), chap. 5; Sacks, "The Widening Gate: Bristol and the Atlantic Economy, 1450–1700" (unpub. ms., Harvard Univ., 1985), chaps. 5, 6, and conclusion.

24 Theodore G. Corbett, "Migration to a Spanish Imperial Frontier in the Seventeenth and Eighteenth Centuries: St. Augustine," *Hispanic American Historical Review*, 54 (1974), 421–425. And see in general three essays in *First Images of America . . .*, ed. Fredi Chiapelli (Berkeley, 1976), vol. II: Woodrow Borah, "The Mixing of Populations"; Peter Boyd-Bowman, "Spanish Emigrants to the Indies, 1595–98: A Profile"; Magnus Mörner, "Spanish Migration to the New World Prior to 1800: A Report on the State of Research."

25 Abel Chatelain, "Les Migrations temporaires françaises au XIXe siècle," *Annales de démographie historique* (1967), 9–28; Chatelain, "Un Type de migration temporaire actuelle: la migration viagère," *Annales: Economies, sociétés, civilisations*, 2 (1947), 411–416; Jean-Pierre Poussou, "Les Mouvements migratoires en France et à partir

de la France de la fin du XVe siècle au début du XIXe siècle: approche pour une synthèse," *Annales de démographie historique* (1970), 11–78.

26 Peter Clark, "The Migrant in Kentish Towns, 1580–1640," in *Crisis and Order,* eds. Clark and Slack, pp. 149, 151–152.

27 The most careful account of the functioning of this system in the seventeenth century is in Clemens, *Eastern Shore,* pp. 20–22, 48–57. See also W. G. Hoskins, "Harvest Fluctuations and English Economic History, 1620–1759," *Agricultural History Review,* 16 (1968), 15–31; Russell R. Menard, "Immigration to the Chesapeake Colonies in the Seventeenth Century . . .," *Maryland Historical Magazine,* 68 (1973), 323–329; David Souden, " 'Rogues, Whores, and Vagabonds': Indentured Servant Emigrants to North America, and the Case of Mid-Seventeenth-Century Bristol," *Social History,* 3 (1978), 23–38; James Horn, "Servant Emigration to the Chesapeake in the Seventeenth Century," in *Chesapeake in the Seventeenth Century,* eds. Tate and Ammerman, chap. 2.

28 The writing on this fundamental transition in American population history is summarized and interpreted in McCusker and Menard, *Economy of British America,* pp. 135–138, and Clemens, *Eastern Shore,* chap. 2; Main, *Tobacco Colony,* pp. 100–106.

29 Bailyn, *Voyagers,* chaps. 2, 14; *The Economic Writings of Francis Horner,* ed. Frank W. Fetter (London, 1957), pp. 120–122. Selkirk himself had touched on the point in his *Observations* (pp. 57–58); Horner developed and explained it.

30 Anon., "Observes or Remarks upon the Lands and Islands which Compose the Barrony Called Harries, the Property of Norman McLeod of McLeod, Esqr," Lee Papers, MS. 3431, f. 180, National Library of Scotland, Edinburgh.

31 For an attempt to draw together part, at least, of the vast literature on German mobility by such prolific German scholars as Werner Hacker, see Bennion, "Flight from the Reich," cited in note 5 above. For a vivid illustration, see Helmut Lahrkamp, "Wanderbewegungen im 18. Jahrhundert: Tiroler Maurer, skandinavische Hutmacher, reisende Buchdrucker, böhmische Glashändler und italienische Kaminfeger in Münster," *Westfälische Forschungen,* 26 (1974), 123–132. On the mobility of the impoverished day laborers of

Mainz, Bonn, and Koblenz, see Etienne François, "Unterschichten und Armut in rheinischen Residenzstädten des 18. Jahrhunderts," *Vierteljahrschrift für Sozial- und Wirtschaftsgeschichte*, 62 (1975), 441–442, 458–459. The migration within and out from the Palatinate has its own important bibliography, much of it emanating from the Heimatstelle Pfalz, a migration research center in Kaiserslautern, whose latest collection of papers, *Pfälzer-Palatines*, ed. Karl Scherer (Kaiserslautern, 1981) contains pieces on the region's mobility, on individual and family experiences in migration, on German folk art in Europe and America, and on German verbal expressions. But such recent publications are only the latest fragments of an immense library of writing on German-American migration history, which, though largely genealogical and antiquarian, can form the basis for a general interpretation of this movement far more revealing than Albert B. Faust's antiquated though still standard account, *The German Element in the United States* (2 vols., Boston and New York, 1909). Emil Meynen's *Bibliography on German Settlements in Colonial North America* (Leipzig, 1937; reprinted Detroit, 1966) lists over 7,500 items, but even when supplemented by the excellent *U.S.A.-Deutschland-Baden und Württemberg* (Gertrud Kuhn, comp., Institut für Auslandsbeziehungen, Stuttgart, 1976) and by Don H. Tolzmann's *German-Americana: A Bibliography* (Metuchen, N.J., 1975), it is still incomplete.

32 Bennion, "Flight from the Reich," chaps. 2, 4; John P. Dern, "London Churchbooks and the German Emigration of 1709," *Schriften zur Wanderungsgeschichte der Pfälzer*, 26 (1968), 17, 36–37.

33 On the Rhineland and the Palatinate as a "Schmelztiegel verschiedener Nationalitäten," see Karl Scherer, "Pfälzer-Palatines: Zur Geschichte der pfälzischen Auswanderung nach Nordamerika," *Stimme der Pfalz*, 27, no. 1 (1976), 4.

34 Scherer, as summarized in Klaus-Peter Westrich, "Symposion 'Pfälzer-Palatines,'" *Pfälzer Heimat*, 27 (1976), 21–22. The term "Palatinate" usually refers to the Rhenish Palatinate, or the Electoral Palatinate *(Kurpfalz)*, an area now divided among the Länder of Rheinland-Pfalz, Baden-Württemberg, and Hessen in the Federal Republic of Germany. The Upper Palatinate *(Oberpfalz)* is now a part of Bavaria.

35 William I. Hull, *William Penn and the Dutch Quaker Migration to Pennsylvania* (Swarthmore, Pa., 1935), pp. 178–179. For the mingling of Dutch and Germans in the border town of Krefeld, the expansion of whose silk industry led to a fivefold increase in population between 1722 and 1763 and in turn to crowding and rising rents and to the emigration of 13 families to Pennsylvania, see Herbert Kisch, "Prussian Mercantilism and the Rise of the Krefeld Silk Industry . . .," *Transactions of the American Philosophical Society*, n.s., 58, pt. 7 (1968).

36 Daniel Häberle, *Auswanderung und Koloniegründungen der Pfälzer im 18. Jahrhundert* (Kaiserslautern, 1909), pp. 147–163.

37 G. E. Kershaw, *The Kennebeck Proprietors, 1749–1775* (Somersworth, N.H., 1975), pp. 71–72; Jasper J. Stahl, *History of Old Broad Bay and Waldoboro* (Portland, Me., 1956), I, 167–168; Charles E. Allen, *History of Dresden, Maine* (p.p., 1931), pp. 135–142.

38 These voluminous records, scattered through innumerable local German archives, have made possible the extensive series of books and articles in German and English detailing, name by name and family by family, the emigrants from particular German communities to the American colonies. The work of several generations of German and American genealogists and historians, of whom the most prominent in recent years has been Professor Donald H. Yoder of the University of Pennsylvania, these scattered writings are descriptive; they only rarely attempt to follow families through from the years before migration to the later years; they attempt no general interpretation; and they separate out the migrants to the west from those who moved east or went to other locations in the surrounding German states. But the best of these publications—such as Yoder's supplemented English edition of Otto Langguth's "Auswanderer aus der Grafschaft Wertheim" [1932] ("Pennsylvania German Pioneers from the County of Wertheim," [*Yearbook of*] *the Pennsylvania German Folklore Society*, XII [1947], 147–289); his similar edition of Adolf Gerber's lists of Württemberg emigrants (*ibid.*, X [1945], 105–237); and his selection from and translation of Heinrich Rembe's *Lambsheim: Die Familien von 1547 bis 1800* . . . (Kaiserslautern, 1971) in *Pennsylvania Folklife*, 23 (1973–74), 40 ff.—reveal remarkably rich sources for reconstructing aspects of

the peopling of early America. Younger historians—such as A. G. Roeber, interpreting the cultural and political consequences of German-American migration in terms of inheritance patterns and concepts of property rights, and Marianne Wokeck, seeking precision in measuring the magnitudes of the eighteenth-century migration—are drawing these scattered German sources into more meaningful patterns, pointing toward a far more sophisticated and important history of the German element in British America than we have had before.

39 Heuchelheim Manumission Protocols, Landesarchiv Speyer, Bestand 2, No. 4595. Karl Heinz Debus, Oberarchivrat of the Landesarchiv Speyer, called my attention to these typical records. The village referred to is in Kreis Frankenthal. Another Heuchelheim, in Kreis Bergzabern, is one of the villages whose population has recently been studied in one of the few sophisticated demographic analyses recently undertaken by German scholars in parallel with the *Annales* community studies in France, the writings of the Cambridge Group in England, and the American studies mentioned in notes 3 and 14 above: Arthur E. Imhof, ed., *Historische Demographie als Sozialgeschichte: Giessen und Umgebung vom 17. zum 19. Jahrhundert* (*Quellen und Forschungen zur hessischen Geschichte,* XXXI, 2 vols., Darmstadt and Marburg, 1975). The success of this project apparently stimulated Imhof and his associates to project a comprehensive rewriting of the whole of German social history through a massive reconstruction of family and community life over the past 400–500 years. For Imhof's account of the racist-oriented genealogical studies of the Nazi period and the work of the Giessen group, see his essay, "Historical Demography as Social History: Possibilities in Germany," *Journal of Family History,* 2 (1977), 305–332.

As can be seen so clearly in the case of Lambsheim, migration studies grow naturally from such sophisticated local histories, and with them comparisons of eighteenth-century German and American communities linked by the migration of identifiable individuals and families. The possibilities are suggested by two American publications, one by a sociologist, the other by a historian: Gillian L. Gollin, *Moravians in Two Worlds* (New York, 1967), and Stephanie G. Wolf, *Urban Village: Population, Community, and Family Structure in Germantown, Pennsylvania, 1683–1800* (Princeton, 1976).

40 Penn, whose colony has been called "the best advertised of all the American colonies," had propaganda agents in London, Dublin, Edinburgh, Hamilton, and Aberdeen; but his chief "correspondence bureau" was in Rotterdam, where his friend, the merchant Benjamin Furly, concentrated on selling the attractions of Pennsylvania throughout the Netherlands and the Rhine Valley. Charles M. Andrews, *Colonial Period of American History* (New Haven, 1934–38), III, 289. On Furly, a remarkable figure—an intellectual as well as a businessman, friend and correspondent of Locke and Sidney, and host in Rotterdam to the leading English political refugees during the crises of the 1670s and '80s—see William I. Hull, *Benjamin Furly and Quakerism in Rotterdam* (Swarthmore, Pa., 1941). On Penn's continental contacts in general, see Hull, *Penn and the Dutch Quaker Migration.*

41 Langguth, "Wertheim," pp. 172–180, 195; John D. Brite, *The Attitude of European States Toward Emigration to the American Colonies . . . 1607–1820* (Chicago, 1939), esp. chap. 4. The active recruitment of emigrants by American and British entrepreneurs in the years immediately preceding the American Revolution is a major theme of my *Voyagers;* their activities are elaborately documented there. For an excellent summary of the expansion of the American economy, see McCusker and Menard, *Economy of British America,* chap. 3. On the increase in non-agricultural employment opportunities for an expanding population as prime land in the eastern areas became scarce, see Duane E. Ball, "Dynamics of Population and Wealth in Eighteenth-century Chester County, Pennsylvania," *Journal of Interdisciplinary History,* 6 (1976), 621–644.

42 Thomas Miller to the Earl of Suffolk, Oct. 25, 1773, Public Record Office (London), SP 54/46, f.248.

43 Bailyn, *Voyagers,* chap. 2; E. R. R. Green, "Queensborough Township: Scotch-Irish Emigration and the Expansion of Georgia, 1763–1776," *W.M.Q.,* 17 (1960), 188. The British government had con-

fronted the problem of emigration as early as the 1720s, with respect to Ireland, but had concluded that "there could be no prohibition of emigration or interference with the level of rents, and henceforth confined itself to fact-finding." Green, "Scotch-Irish Emigration, an Imperial Problem," *Western Pennsylvania Historical Magazine*, 35 (1952), 198–200.

44 Langguth, "Wertheim," pp. 169–170, 180; Brite, *Attitude of European States*, chap. 6.

45 E. A. Wrigley and R. S. Schofield, *The Population History of England, 1541–1871* (Cambridge, Mass., 1981), p. 175.

46 Edward M. Riley, ed., *The Journal of John Harrower . . . 1773–1776* (Williamsburg, Va., and New York, 1963).

I I
The Rings of Saturn

1 Philip F. Gura, *A Glimpse of Sion's Glory: Puritan Radicalism in New England, 1620–1660* (Middletown, Conn., 1984); David S. Lovejoy, *Religious Enthusiasm in the New World* (Cambridge, Mass., 1985), chaps. 3–6.

2 Bailyn, *The New England Merchants in the Seventeenth Century* (Cambridge, Mass., 1955), chap. 7; Bailyn, "The Blount Papers: Notes on the Merchant 'Class' in the Revolutionary Period," *W.M.Q.*, 11 (1954), 98–104; Arthur L. Jensen, *The Maritime Commerce of Colonial Philadelphia* (Madison, Wis., 1963), chap. 13.

3 A. S. Eisenstadt, *Charles McLean Andrews* (New York, 1956), chap. 1, for the importance of New England town studies in Adams's time; Michael Zuckerman, *Peaceable Kingdoms* (New York, 1970); Edward M. Cook, Jr., *The Fathers of the Towns: Leadership and Community Structure in Eighteenth-Century New England* (Baltimore, 1976). Quotations from T. H. Breen, "Persistent Localism: English Social Change and the Shaping of New England Institutions," *W.M.Q.*, 32 (1975), 17–28; Stephen Innes, *Labor in a New Land: Economy and Society in Seventeenth-century Springfield* (Princeton, 1983), p. xvi.

4 Rough classifications of settlement patterns have been available for many years (e.g., Glenn T. Trewartha, "Types of Rural Settlement in Colonial America," *Geographical Review*, 36 [1946], 568–596), but since Lois K. Mathews's Turnerian *Expansion of New England* (Boston, 1909) there has been no attempt to sketch generally New England's internal migration history, and only very recently has a start been made on analyzing any of these movements in demographic terms. An interesting nonstatistical effort to trace one small area of movement through genealogical records is Ralph J. Crandall, "New England's Second Great Migration: The First Three Generations of Settlement, 1630–1700," *New England Historical and Genealogical Register*, 129 (1975), 347–360. Doris O'Keefe, "Marriage and Migration in Colonial New England: A Study in Historical Population Geography" (Discussion Paper no. 16, Department of Geography, Syracuse Univ., 1976), shows by an examination of the vital statistics of seven eastern Massachusetts towns an initial "tendency towards rootedness" in the first and second generations; an increasing incidence of marriage migration (women three times more commonly than men); a limited range of geographical movement involved in such marriages (90 percent within a radius of 50 miles, over 50 percent within 15 miles); and an emerging role of the older, centrally located towns as "marriage centers." Similarly, Susan L. Norton, "Marital Migration in Essex County, Massachusetts . . .," *Journal of Marriage and the Family*, 35 (1973), 406–418, examining marriages in six Essex County towns, finds longer distances involved in marriage migrations than have been found for English and Italian marriages; a strong tendency to draw marriage partners from the less-populated northern districts of New England; and significant differences between male and female mobility patterns. Migration and settlement patterns and endogamy rates in marriage are central aspects of the extensive study of the early population of the upper Connecticut River Valley being carried out by members of the Anthropology Department at the University of Massachusetts, Amherst. Their preliminary findings support those of O'Keefe and Norton: Alan Swedlund *et al.*, "Population Studies in the Connecticut Valley: Prospectus," *Journal of Human Evolution*, 5 (1976), 75–93. For other aspects of migration and community differentiation see Douglas L.

Jones, "The Strolling Poor . . .," *Journal of Social History*, 8 (1974), 28–54; H. Roger King, "The Settlement of the Upper Connecticut River Valley to 1675" (Ph.D. diss., Vanderbilt Univ., 1965); and Robert L. Goodman, "The New England Origins of Woodbridge, N.J., 1635–1685: A Study of Kinship and Friendship Patterns" (Ph.D. diss., Michigan State Univ., 1973).

5 James A. Henretta, "The Morphology of New England Society in the Colonial Period," *Journal of Interdisciplinary History*, 2 (1971), 379–398.

6 Darrett B. Rutman, "People in Process: The New Hampshire Towns of the Eighteenth Century," *Journal of Urban History*, 1 (1975), 268–292.

7 Richard Pillsbury, "The Urban Street Pattern as a Culture Indicator: Pennsylvania, 1682–1815," *Annals of the Association of American Geographers*, 60 (1970), 428–446.

8 Carville V. Earle, "The First English Towns of North America," *Geographical Review*, 67 (1977), 34–50 (explaining the origins—not the development—of colonial towns and the character of urban life in terms of immigrant flows and the needs of immigrants in frontier communities); Jacob M. Price, "Economic Function and the Growth of American Port Towns in the Eighteenth Century," *Perspectives in American History*, 8 (1974), 123–186 (explaining the varieties of eighteenth-century towns in terms of varying marketing functions in Atlantic commerce); and Earle and Ronald Hoffman, "Staple Crops and Urban Development in the Eighteenth-Century South," *ibid.*, pp. 7–78 (arguing that the determinant of urban growth in the south was the nature of the staple crops produced in the hinterlands).

9 Lemuel Shattuck, *Report to the Committee of the City Council Appointed to Obtain the Census of Boston for the Year 1845* (Boston, 1846), pp. 2–5; John B. Blake, *Public Health in the Town of Boston 1630–1822* (Cambridge, 1959), pp. 247–249; Ralph J. Crandall, "New England's Haven Port: Charlestown and Her Restless People, A Study of Colonial Migration, 1629–1775" (Ph.D. diss., Univ. of Southern California, 1975), pp. 188 ff., esp. 192–193. In a working paper, "On the Problem of Boston's Population Growth in the Mid-Eighteenth Century" (1977), summarizing and interpreting

the existing writing on Boston's population in the colonial period, Lee Shai Weissbach places Boston's history in the wider context of a general exodus from eastern New England to newly opened lands in western New England after 1740, suggesting that "it was not Boston's population alone which failed to grow at the rate prevailing for the colony as a whole, but the population of the older and better established towns of eastern New England generally." He also examines the likelihood of an internal shift in the town's population, as certain elements left the town for other communities while poorer transients entered, to compete for the available jobs. For suggestions of Boston's role in marriage mobility, see O'Keefe paper, cited above, note 4.

10 For the use of this term in a broad context, see Aristide R. Zolberg, "International Migration Policies in a Changing World System," in *Human Migration: Patterns and Policies*, ed. William H. McNeill and Ruth S. Adams (Bloomington, Ind., 1978), p. 257. On Philadelphia's growth in the pre-Revolutionary years, see Sharon V. Salinger and Charles Wetherell, "A Note on the Population of Pre-revolutionary Philadelphia," *Pennsylvania Magazine of History and Biography*, 109 (1985), 369–386, esp. Table 7.

11 *Wöchentliche Pennsylvanische Staatsbote*, Dec. 14, 28, 1773; Feb. 8, 1774. See also *Pennsylvania Gazette*, Jan. 12, Feb. 9, and Feb. 23, 1774.

12 Billy G. Smith, "Death and Life in a Colonial Immigrant City: A Demographic Analysis of Philadelphia," *Journal of Economic History*, 37 (1977), 863–889; Gary B. Nash, "Poverty and Poor Relief in Pre-Revolutionary Philadelphia," *W.M.Q.*, 33 (1976), 12–14, 22, 28; Nash, *The Urban Crucible* (Cambridge, Mass., 1979), pp. 103, 106, 127, 178–179, 247–248, 254–256. For a medical description of the immigrants' diseases and their spread through the city, see Roslyn S. Wolman, "Some Aspects of Community Health in Colonial Philadelphia" (Ph.D. diss., University of Pennsylvania, 1974); chap. 2 traces the story chronologically and describes the evolution of quarantine regulations. The low level of poverty in Philadelphia before 1760, even when immigrants were flooding into the city, is quite remarkable; and indeed even later, in the depressed years after 1763, only 5 percent of the population received poor relief. Even if one includes everyone who could reasonably be described as a recipient

of the city's charity in any form, the figure appears to be about 7 percent—a very small percentage in comparison with equivalent figures for European cities of this size. The idea that there were progressive and profound impoverishment and immiseration among the lower strata in the eighteenth-century American towns, leading to conditions equivalent to those in the British cities, has been challenged; for a summary of these views, see John J. McCusker and Russell R. Menard, *The Economy of British America, 1607–1789* (Chapel Hill, N.C., 1985), pp. 254, 271–276. For some figures on the continuing disappearance from Philadelphia of the overwhelming percentage of the city's poor, many if not most of whom were immigrants who relocated themselves elsewhere in the colonies, see Gary Nash, "Up From the Bottom in Franklin's Philadelphia," *Past & Present*, 77 (1977), pp. 67–68.

13 Bailyn, *Voyagers to the West* (New York, 1986), chap. 16.

14 In 1963 the Kassel, West Germany, publisher Bärenreiter issued a facsimile edition of Merian's *Topographia Germaniae*, 2d ed. (1672). The volume entitled *Topographia Palatinatus Rheni* . . . contains scenes of the villages and towns from which many of the emigrants to America left.

15 E. Estyn Evans, "The Scotch-Irish: Their Cultural Adaptation and Heritage in the American Old West," in E. R. R. Green, ed., *Essays in Scotch-Irish History* (New York, 1969), pp. 73–76. For a particularly vivid and exact depiction of the distribution and community-settlement patterns of the German sectarians (Amish, Dunkard, Mennonite, and Schwenkfelder), see C. Lee Hopple, "Spatial Development of the Southeastern Pennsylvania Plain Dutch Community to 1970," *Pennsylvania Folklife*, 21, no. 2 (1971–1972), 18–40; 21, no. 3 (1972), 36–45. For a general picture of ethnic and religious population flows and settlement patterns in Pennsylvania, see James T. Lemon, *The Best Poor Man's Country* (Baltimore, 1972), chap. 3; for the resulting diversity, Sally Schwartz, " 'A Mixed Multitude': Religion and Ethnicity in Colonial Pennsylvania" (Ph.D. diss., Harvard Univ., 1981). For a parallel account of ethnic distribution in North Carolina, see Harry R. Merrens, *Colonial North Carolina in the Eighteenth Century* (Chapel Hill, N.C., 1964),

chap. 4; for the Shenandoah Valley, Robert D. Mitchell, *Commercialism and Frontier: Perspectives on the Early Shenandoah Valley* (Charlottesville, Va., 1977), chaps. 2, 4.

16 Henry A. Gemery, "Emigration from the British Isles to the New World, 1630–1700: Inferences from Colonial Populations," in *Research in Economic History*, 5 (1980), esp. pp. 196–197; David W. Galenson, *White Servitude in Colonial America: An Economic Analysis* (Cambridge, Eng., 1981), esp. chap. 3; Mildred Campbell, "Social Origins of Some Early Americans," in *Seventeenth-Century America*, ed. James M. Smith (Chapel Hill, N.C., 1959); David Souden, " 'Rogues, Whores, and Vagabonds': Indentured Servant Emigrants to North America, and the Case of Mid-Seventeenth-Century Bristol," *Social History*, 3 (1978), 23–41; James Horn, "Servant Emigration to the Chesapeake in the Seventeenth Century," in *The Chesapeake in the Seventeenth Century*, ed. Thad W. Tate and David L. Ammerman (New York, 1979). For a summary of the current controversy over the social origins of the labor force recruited as immigrants, see McCusker and Menard, *Economy of British America*, pp. 242–243.

17 Henry A. Gemery, "European Emigration to North America, 1700–1820: Numbers and Quasi-Numbers," *Perspectives in American History*, new ser., 1 (1984), 283–342; Galenson, *White Servitude*, chaps. 4, 8, 9; A. Roger Ekirch, "Bound for America: A Profile of British Convicts Transported to the Colonies, 1718–1775," *W.M.Q.*, 42 (1985), p. 188; Marianne Wokeck, "The Flow and the Composition of German Immigration to Philadelphia, 1727–1775," *Pennsylvania Magazine of History and Biography*, 105 (1981), 249–278; Bailyn, *Voyagers*, Part III. No general account of the German immigration of the eighteenth century outside of Pennsylvania has been written since A. B. Faust's long-outdated *German Element in the United States* (Boston and New York, 1909), but for an exhaustive account of their settlement in one area outside of Pennsylvania, see Winthrop P. Bell, *The "Foreign Protestants" and the Settlement of Nova Scotia* (Toronto, 1961).

18 Philip Fendell to James Russell, Port Tobacco, Md., Aug. 26, 1774, James Russell Papers (Coutts & Co., London; microfilm copy in

Alderman Library, Univ. of Virginia, Charlottesville); Thomas Smyth to James Cheston, Langford's Bay, Md., March 30, 1774, James Cheston Incoming Letters, Cheston-Galloway Papers (Maryland Hall of Records, Annapolis); James & Drinker to Capt. Edward Spain, Philadelphia, Aug. 4, 1774, James & Drinker Foreign Letters, Drinker Papers (Historical Society of Pennsylvania, Philadelphia).

19 Abbot E. Smith, *Colonists in Bondage: White Servitude and Convict Labor in America, 1607–1776* (Chapel Hill, N.C., 1947), pp. 288–289; Bailyn, *Voyagers*, Table 5.15.

20 Charles S. Grant, "Land Speculation and the Settlement of Kent, 1738–1760," *New England Quarterly*, 28 (1955), 51–54, more fully developed in Grant's *Democracy in the Connecticut Frontier Town of Kent* (New York, 1961). The Turnerian interpretation of the role of land speculation in the movement of the frontier was developed by Ray A. Billington: "The Origin of the Land Speculator as a Frontier Type," *Agricultural History*, 19 (1945), 204–212. Billington's interpretation rests on the great wealth of scholarship in western history that followed in Turner's wake, but it is implicit in Turner's original formulation of frontier history. See also, for an important overview in these terms, Paul W. Gates, "The Role of the Land Speculator in Western Development," *Pennsylvania Magazine of History and Biography*, 66 (1942), 314–333.

21 John F. Martin has uncovered an extraordinary mass of evidence of land speculation in the initial establishment of the Puritan towns of New England; in town after town commercial interests preceded religious: "Entrepreneurship and the Founding of New England Towns: The Seventeenth Century" (Ph.D. diss., Harvard Univ., 1985).

22 Edith M. Fox, *Land Speculation in the Mohawk Country* (Ithaca, N.Y., 1949), p. 3; Aubrey C. Land, "Economic Behavior in a Planting Society: The Eighteenth-Century Chesapeake," *Journal of Southern History*, 33 (1967), 480; Rowland Berthoff and John M. Murrin, "Feudalism, Communalism, and the Yeoman Freeholder . . .," in *Essays on the American Revolution*, ed. Stephen G. Kurtz and James H. Hutson (Chapel Hill, N.C., 1973), 265 ff.; Charles G. Sellers, Jr., "Private Profits and British Colonial Policy:

The Speculations of Henry McCulloh," *W.M.Q.,* 8 (1951), 535–551;
Fox, *Land Speculation;* Catherine S. Crary, "The American Dream:
John Tabor Kempe's Rise from Poverty to Riches," *W.M.Q.,* 14
(1957), 176–196; Richard L. Morton, *Colonial Virginia* (Chapel Hill,
N.C., 1960), II, chaps, 1–8; Aubrey C. Land, "A Land Speculator
[Daniel Dulany] in the Opening of Western Maryland," *Maryland
Historical Magazine,* 48 (1953), 191–203; R. Bruce Harley, "Dr.
Charles Carroll—Land Speculator, 1730–1755," *ibid.,* 46 (1951), 93–
107; *The Prose Works of William Byrd of Westover,* ed. Louis B.
Wright (Cambridge, Mass., 1966), pp. 10, 28–29, 31–32, 339 n.;
Wright, *The First Gentlemen of Virginia* (San Marino, Calif., 1940),
pp. 346–347, 248–249, 259; *The Diary of Colonel Landon Carter of
Sabine Hall, 1752–1778,* ed. Jack P. Greene (Charlottesville, Va.,
1965), I, 4–6; Patricia U. Bonomi, *A Factious People: Politics and
Society in Colonial New York* (New York, 1971), chap. 3, esp. pp.
66–68, chap. 4, esp. pp. 186–187.

23 Grant, "Land Speculation . . . Kent," p. 55. For parallel activities
in newly opened areas of the Virginia piedmont, see S. Edward
Ayres, "Albemarle County, 1744–1770: An Economic, Political, and
Social Analysis," *Magazine of Albemarle County History,* 25 (1966–
1967), 48–50, which describes the widespread small-scale speculation of settlers of moderate means.

24 Billington, "Land Speculator," p. 207; Theodore B. Lewis, "Land
Speculation and the Dudley Council of 1686," *W.M.Q.,* 31 (1974),
pp. 255–272.

25 Russell R. Menard, "From Servant to Freeholder . . .," *W.M.Q.,* 30
(1973), 37–64; Menard, "Opportunity and Inequality . . . 1638–1705,"
Maryland Historical Magazine, 69 (1974), 169–184; Abbot E. Smith,
"The Indentured Servant and Land Speculation in Seventeenth
Century Maryland," *American Historical Review,* 40 (1935), 467–472;
Land, "Economic Behavior," p. 481, n. 30.

26 Mitchell, *Commercialism and Frontier,* chaps. 2, 3.

27 Walter A. Knittle, *The Early Eighteenth Century Palatine Emigration* (Philadelphia, 1936), chaps. 5–8.

28 The importation of servants was a lucrative though limited sideline
for American merchants and shipowners, providing valuable
"freight" that could be sold for cash. Only in the case of German

immigrants did the trade reach sizable proportions, involving major Dutch shippers and leading Philadelphia importers. For an excellent example of the operation of the servant trade, see Grace H. Larson, "Profile of a Colonial Merchant: Thomas Clifford of Pre-Revolutionary Philadelphia" (Ph.D. diss., Columbia Univ., 1955), pp. 110–124. (I am grateful to Thomas Doerflinger for this reference and for a suggestive discussion of the whole subject, summarizing part of his work in progress on the Philadelphia merchants in the Revolutionary era.)

29 Erna Risch, "Joseph Crellius, Immigrant Broker," *New England Quarterly*, 12 (1939), 241–267; G. E. Kershaw, *Kennebeck Proprietors, 1749–1775* (Somersworth, N.H., 1975), chap. 4; John D. Brite, *The Attitude of European States toward Emigration to the American Colonies . . . 1607–1820* (Chicago, 1939), pp. 140–143; Cyrus Eaton, *Annals of the Town of Warren; with . . . the Waldo Patent* (Hallowell, Maine, 1851), pp. 80–86; Charles E. Allen, *History of Dresden, Maine* (n.p., 1931), chap. 11. Waldo's circular advertising his lands to the Germans, typical of many such documents, dated Frankfurt, 1753, is printed in *Collections of the Maine Historical Society*, VI (1859), pp. 325–332. For an interesting paper by James Bowdoin, entitled, "Some Thoughts on the Importation of Foreigners: To Encourage It" (c. 1748), which was part of the effort to involve the government in recruitment, see Bowdoin-Temple Papers, II (Massachusetts Historical Society, Boston).

30 E. R. R. Green, "Queensborough Township: Scotch-Irish Emigration and the Expansion of Georgia, 1763–1776," *W.M.Q.*, 17 (1960), 184 ff. It has been argued forcefully that the failure of population growth in Georgia during the trustees' control was due to economic policies that limited land acquisition in large parcels and in fee simple, thus effectively eliminating land speculation. Milton L. Ready, "Land Tenure in Trusteeship Georgia," *Agricultural History*, 48 (1974), 353–368. For Governor Gooch's argument, in 1728, that the granting of large tracts to "men of substance" was necessary to advance settlement, see *Calendar of State Papers, Colonial Series, America and West Indies*, XXXVI (1728–1729), ed. Cecil Headlam (London, 1937), #446. For the energetic recruitment of Ger-

mans and Scots to settle on the estates of the Livingstons, Verplancks, Johnsons, Duanes, and other large landowners in New York, see Sung Bok Kim, "A New Look at the Great Landlords of Eighteenth-Century New York," *W.M.Q.*, 27 (1970), 600–603. On land speculation and the promotion of Scotch-Irish emigration, see R. J. Dickson, *Ulster Emigration to Colonial America, 1718–1775* (1966; rpt., Antrim, 1976), chap. 8.

31 The text of the "Additional Instructions" of February 1774 is printed in *Royal Instructions to British Colonial Governors, 1670–1776*, ed. Leonard W. Labaree (New York, 1935), II, 533–537; Pownall's explanation is enclosure 3 of his letter to Lord Dartmouth, Nov. 6, 1773, in Dartmouth Papers, MG 23, A1, III, 3469–3476 (Public Archives of Canada, Ottawa).

32 Ian C. C. Graham, *Colonists from Scotland: Emigration to North America, 1707–1783* (Ithaca, N.Y., 1956), pp. 81–88.

33 Details of large-scale land speculation and associated migration schemes in the Floridas and Nova Scotia are traced in Bailyn, *Voyagers*, chaps. 11–13. The quotations in the paragraphs that follow are documented there.

34 *Newcastle Journal*, April 2–9, 1774. For a sketch of the spectacular and catastrophic importation of Greeks, North Italians, and Minorcans to the settlement at New Smyrna, on Mosquito Inlet, East Florida, see pp. 129–31 of the present work.

35 For the view "that most leaseholders viewed tenancy as a temporary condition—as a way station on the road to independency" (Bonomi), there is substantial documentation for every region and period of the colonial era. On the mutual benefit to landlords and tenants of short-term rentals in Maryland in the 1640s and '50s— tenancy enabling the landless "to accumulate the capital necessary to acquire a tract of their own"—see Menard, "From Servant to Freeholder," pp. 52–54. Menard's view that tenancy became "a permanent fate" in the later seventeenth century (p. 60 n. 76) is less fully substantiated. Bailyn, *Voyagers*, Parts IV and V (esp. chap. 11) has many such examples, as does Eugene R. Fingerhut's study, "Assimilation of Immigrants on the Frontier of New York, 1764– 1776" (Ph.D. diss., Columbia Univ., 1962), esp. pp. 130–132, 172, 213. For

illustrations of the general point in other writings on the eighteenth
century, see Fox, *Land Speculation,* pp. 10–11, 42–47; Bonomi, *Factious People,* pp. 196–200; Mitchell, *Commercialism and Frontier,* pp.
78–84; Kim, "Great Landlords," pp. 581–614; Armand La Potin,
"The Minisink Grant . . .," *New York History,* 56 (1975), 29–50; and
Ayres, "Albemarle County," pp. 45, 49. At times tenancy became so
attenuated from its traditional form that it is difficult to distinguish it
from independent landownership. Thus the settlers of Lancaster,
Pennsylvania, were technically "tenants" of Andrew Hamilton,
who had bought the area on speculation. But in fact all they owed
him was a small "ground rent," equivalent to a tax, and even that
most of them refused to pay. Jerome H. Wood, Jr., "The Town
Proprietors of Lancaster, 1730–1790," *Pennsylvania Magazine of History and Biography,* 96 (1972), 346–368. For an identical situation in
the Cherry Valley patent on the Mohawk in New York, see Fox,
Land Speculation, pp. 43–44. The Calverts in Maryland promoted
the use of "developmental leases" "to develop previously uncultivated land into working farms and plantations so that the rental or
sale value of the tract would be increased. Ideally, developmental
leasing benefited both landlord and tenant. The tenant received a
tract of land for a low annual rent, and the landlord could charge
much higher rents when the first lease expired, counterbalancing the
years of small income from the developmental lease." Gregory A.
Stiverson, *Poverty in a Land of Plenty* (Baltimore, 1977), p. 10.

36 Land, "A Land Speculator," pp. 196–198; some details on "Tasker's
Chance" drawn from Lee Shai Weissbach, "The Peopling of West-
ern Maryland" (working paper, Harvard Univ., 1977); Edward P.
Alexander, *A Revolutionary Conservative: James Duane of New York*
(New York, 1938), pp. 58–59. For other examples of similar strate-
gies, see Kim, "Great Landlords," p. 597.

37 Innes, *Labor in a New Land,* chap. 3; Stiverson, *Poverty in a Land
of Plenty,* esp. chap. 5; Willard F. Bliss, "The Rise of Tenancy in
Virginia," *Virginia Magazine of History and Biography,* 58 (1950),
427–441. Stiverson's book presents a complex picture. The proprietor's sale of his tenanted lands was a failure. The tenants either
could not or would not bid for the property, but neither did outsid-
ers, and so there were few sales and "the majority of the land on

the manors remained in the possession of the tenants at the conclusion of the proprietary sales" (p. 108). The land was finally sold as confiscated loyalist property during the Revolution; but even then, when speculation was rampant, there was relatively little dislocation of the original tenants. The Revolution ended widespread tenancy in Maryland, and Stiverson sees the apex of the institution in the late colonial period. But whether the spread of tenancy and its stability in several regions in that period were the results of widespread poverty that kept tenants from acquiring freeholds, or whether "tenants did not aspire to become freeholders," is unclear (p. 140). In some areas tenants were affluent and could have acquired freehold property if they had wanted to; in others, they were impoverished dirt farmers living in squalor. In the one case, long-term tenancy was a reasonable economic strategy since rents were low; in the other, the farms were so unprofitable that the rents were scarcely worth collecting. In neither situation did tenancy in Maryland duplicate the form and function of tenancy in traditional societies. The average total income per year that accrued to the proprietor from the rental of almost 200,000 acres of manors and reserves, 1752–1761, was £750 stg. (p. 18).

I I I

A Domesday Book
for the Periphery

1 Richard S. Dunn, *Puritans and Yankees: The Winthrop Dynasty of New England, 1630–1717* (Princeton, 1962), traces this three-generational transition with great care: the treatment of the second and third generations is especially sensitive and revealing. For the attenuation of Puritan culture through the next two generations, see Richard L. Bushman, *From Puritan to Yankee: Character and the Social Order in Connecticut, 1690–1765* (Cambridge, Mass., 1967).

2 Daniel S. Smith, "The Demographic History of Colonial New

England," *Journal of Economic History*, 32 (1972), 165–183; Kenneth
A. Lockridge, "The Population of Dedham, Massachusetts, 1636–
1736," *Economic History Review*, 2d ser., 19 (1966), 318–344. Lockridge's conclusions are heavily qualified by a broader analysis by
Mary Dobson, "From the Old World to the New World—A Transition in Mortality" (unpublished paper, Harvard Univ., 1979),
which contrasts the demographic history of colonial New England
with that of selected communities in Kent, England. The ravages
of disease may have been worse in eighteenth-century New England than in southern England. Township figures are derived
from a working paper and accompanying maps by Lee Shai Weissbach, Harvard Univ., 1977.

3 Philip J. Greven, Jr., *Four Generations: Population, Land, and Family in Colonial Andover, Massachusetts* (Ithaca, N.Y., 1970), esp.
chaps. 5–8.

4 Thomas J. Archdeacon, *New York City, 1664–1710: Conquest and
Change* (Ithaca, N.Y., 1976), esp. chap. 2 (quotation at 33); Patricia
U. Bonomi, *A Factious People: Politics and Society in Colonial New
York* (New York, 1971), esp. chap. 2.

5 Peter O. Wacker, *Land and People, A Cultural Geography of Preindustrial New Jersey: Origins and Settlement Patterns* (New Brunswick, N.J., 1975), chap. 3; Ned C. Landsman, *Scotland and Its First
American Colony 1683–1763* (Princeton, 1985), chaps. 4–6; Sally
Schwartz, " 'A Mixed Multitude': Religion and Ethnicity in Colonial Pennsylvania" (Ph.D. diss., Harvard Univ., 1981), esp. chaps.
3–5; James T. Lemon, *The Best Poor Man's Country: A Geographical
Study of Early Southeastern Pennsylvania* (Baltimore, 1972), chaps.
1–3; Gary B. Nash, *Quakers and Politics: Pennsylvania, 1681–1726*
(Princeton, 1968), p. 174. On Leisler's Rebellion, besides Archdeacon, *New York City*, chap. 5, see Jerome R. Reich, *Leisler's Rebellion: A Study of Democracy in New York, 1664–1720* (Chicago, 1953).
On the emerging aristocracies, see Bonomi, *Factious People*, chaps.
2, 3; Archdeacon, *New York City*, chaps. 3, 4; Frederick B. Tolles,
Meeting House and Counting House: The Quaker Merchants of Colonial Philadelphia (Chapel Hill, N.C., 1948).

6 For a summary of the now extensive literature on Chesapeake

population history in the seventeenth century, see John J. McCusker and Russell R. Menard, *The Economy of British America, 1607–1789* (Chapel Hill, N.C., 1985), pp. 133–143, 236–257, and writings cited there. On Gloria Main, *Tobacco Colony: Life in Early Maryland, 1650–1720* (Princeton, 1982), and Darrett B. Rutman and Anita H. Rutman, *A Place in Time: Middlesex County, Virginia, 1650–1750* (New York, 1984), see above, chap. 1, note 14. See also Edmund S. Morgan, *American Slavery, American Freedom* (New York, 1975), chaps. 7–15, and Paul G. Clemens, *The Atlantic Economy and Colonial Maryland's Eastern Shore* (Ithaca, N.Y., 1980), chaps. 1–3. The shift in the composition of the labor force is analyzed in David W. Galenson, *White Servitude in Colonial America: An Economic Analysis* (Cambridge, Eng., 1981), chaps. 8, 9; for the figures cited, see Main, *Tobacco Colony*, p. 100, and Main, "Maryland and the Chesapeake Economy, 1670–1720," in *Law, Society, and Politics in Early Maryland*, eds. Aubrey C. Land *et al.* (Baltimore, 1977), 134–135.

7 *The Prose Works of William Byrd of Westover*, ed. Louis B. Wright (Cambridge, Mass., 1966), intro.; Ivor Noël Hume, *Here Lies Virginia* (New York, 1963), pp. 139–142; Thomas T. Waterman and John A. Barrows, *Domestic Colonial Architecture of Tidewater Virginia* (New York, 1968), pp. 12–13.

8 Louis B. Wright, *The First Gentlemen of Virginia* (San Marino, Calif., 1940), p. 191 and chap. 6; Rutman and Rutman, *Place in Time*, pp. 153–156, 211–214, 220; *William Fitzhugh and His Chesapeake World, 1676–1701*, ed. Richard B. David (Chapel Hill, N.C., 1963), pp. 18, 14–15, 175–176; Henry Hartwell, James Blair, and Edward Chilton, *The Present State of Virginia, and the College* [*1697*], ed. Hunter D. Farish (Williamsburg, Va., 1940), p. 8; Main, *Tobacco Colony*, pp. 261, 153, 141.

9 *Ibid.*, p. 140; Hartwell *et al.*, *Present State*, p. 14.

10 Elizabeth C. Vann and Margaret C. Dixon, *Virginia's First German Colony* (Richmond, Va., 1961); John W. Wayland, *Germanna . . . 1714–1956* (Staunton, Va., 1956), pp. 10–21.

11 Thomas J. Wertenbaker, *The Planters of Colonial Virginia* (Princeton, 1922), p. 57 and appendix; *Memoirs of a Huguenot Family*, ed. Ann Maury (New York, 1972), p. 264.

12 Hugh T. Lefler and William S. Powell, *Colonial North Carolina* (New York, 1973), chaps. 2, 3.

13 Peter H. Wood, *Black Majority* (New York, 1974), chaps. 1, 2, 4, p. 106; *The Carolina Chronicle of Dr. Francis Le Jau, 1706–1717*, ed. Frank T. Klingberg (Berkeley, 1956), p. 55; Mary Stafford to [?] [South Carolina], Aug. 23, 1711, in *South Carolina Historical Magazine*, 81 (1980), 4.

14 Verner W. Crane, *The Southern Frontier, 1670–1732* (Durham, N.C., 1928), chaps. 5, 6 (figures at p. 111).

15 Denys Hay, "England, Scotland and Europe: The Problem of the Frontier," *Transactions of the Royal Historical Society*, 5th ser., 25 (1975), 77–91, quotation at p. 82.

16 William Blackstone, *Commentaries on the Laws of England*, 3d ed. (Oxford, 1768), bk. I, chap. 14, i; *The Eighteenth-Century Constitution, 1688–1815*, ed. E. Neville Williams (Cambridge, Eng., 1960), pp. 387–388.

17 Alonzo Quint, ed., "Journal of the Rev. John Pike," *Proceedings of the Massachusetts Historical Society*, 14 (1875–1876), 149, 131; *Puritans among the Indians: Accounts of Captivity and Redemption, 1676–1724*, ed. Alden T. Vaughan and Edward W. Clark (Cambridge, Mass., 1981), p. 163; James Axtell, *The European and the Indian* (Oxford, 1981), chaps. 2, 8.

18 *The Colonial and State Records of North Carolina*, ed. William L. Saunders *et al.* (Raleigh, etc., 1886–1914), I, 827; Richard M. Brown, *The South Carolina Regulators* (Cambridge, Mass., 1963), pp. 7, 12.

19 Alden T. Vaughan and Daniel K. Richter, "Crossing the Cultural Divide: Indians and New Englanders, 1605–1763," *Proceedings of the American Antiquarian Society*, 90, pt. 1 (1980), 53–95, traces the fates of 1,641 New England prisoners of the Indians and French, only 754 of whom are known to have seen their homes again.

20 The literature on the captivity narratives is extensive. See esp. the introduction to the excellent collection *Puritans Among the Indians;* Roy H. Pearce, "The Significances of the Captivity Narratives," *American Literature*, 19 (1947), 1–20; and David L. Minter, "By Dens of Lions . . .," *ibid.*, 45 (1973), 335–347. The psychological impact of

these writings is extremely difficult to grasp. For one attempt to penetrate these inner experiences, see Richard Slotkin, *Regeneration through Violence: The Mythology of the American Frontier, 1600–1860* (Middletown, Conn., 1977), chaps. 4–6.

21 Gov. Gabriel Johnston to Lord Wilmington, Brompton, on Cape Fear River, Feb. 10, 1737, W. R. Coe Papers, South Carolina Historical Society (Charleston, S.C.); Bernard Romans, *A Concise Natural History of East and West Florida* . . . [1775], reprint ed. (New Orleans, 1961), p. 41 (cf. Romans's "An Attempt towards a Short Description of West Florida," in *Publications of the Mississippi Historical Society,* V [1925], 180: a "vile race . . . the very savages are scandalized at the lives of those brutes in human shapes"); James Habersham to James Wright, Aug. 20, 1772, *Letters of Hon. James Habersham, 1756–1775 (Collections of the Georgia Historical Society,* VI, Savannah, 1904), 203–204; *Belfast [Ireland] News Letter,* Feb. 12, 1768; Marc B. Fried, *The Early History of Kingston & Ulster County, N.Y.* (Kingston, N.Y., 1975); "De Graffenried's Manuscript . . .," in *Colonial and State Records of North Carolina,* I, 905 ff.; Richard J. Hooker, ed., *The Carolina Backcountry on the Eve of the Revolution* (Chapel Hill, 1953); Brown, *South Carolina Regulators,* chap. 2; Albert T. Volwiler, *George Croghan and the Westward Movement, 1741–1782* (Cleveland, 1926), p. 214. For a vivid account of disorder and violence on the Kentucky frontier associated through kinship with Jefferson, see Boynton Merrill, Jr., *Jefferson's Nephews* (Princeton, 1976).

22 *The Secret Diary of William Byrd of Westover, 1709–1712,* ed. Louis B. Wright and Marion Tinling (Richmond, Va., 1941), pp. 2, 15, 46, 79, 84, 112, 113, 127, 192, 205, 307, 419, 494, 551, 564.

23 Wright, *First Gentlemen,* chap. 11; *The Carolina Chronicle of Dr. Francis Le Jau,* pp. 78, 55, 129, 130, 108, 61; *The Diary of Colonel Landon Carter of Sabine Hall, 1752–1778,* ed. Jack P. Greene (Charlottesville, Va., 1965).

24 Stephen S. Webb, *The Governors-General: The English Army and the Definition of the Empire, 1569–1681* (Chapel Hill, N.C., 1979), esp. chap. 1, Conclusion, and Epilogue; *Calendar of State Papers, Colonial Series, 1574–1660,* ed. W. Noel Sainsbury (London, 1860), p. 12,

cited in David Konig, "Criminal Justice in the New World: English Anticipations and the Virginia Experience in the Sixteenth and Seventeenth Centuries," forthcoming in *American Journal of Legal History*. Konig concludes: "By the mid-seventeenth century, a long and well-established tradition in the hinterlands had demonstrated the advantages of swift and discretionary justice and the attenuation of common law rights for preserving public order and securing the state against internal opposition. Colonial transportation and penal servitude were the logical continuation of that process, for what could no longer be done in England after the revolutions of the seventeenth century could—indeed, *had to*—be done beyond the seas. Government in London, both Crown and Parliament, saw that England's insoluble problems of social order could be transplanted and handled by methods that once had served the purposes of state-building in England but now had become politically objectionable. As Elizabethans thought to send incorrigible rogues to some far-off and indeterminate area known as 'Virginia,' so, too, did a Restoration Parliament think to banish 'seditious sectaries and other disloyal persons' to the West Indies. The usefulness of colonial transportation was too great to be abandoned by an English criminal justice system unable to deal with such intractables." On the transportation of convicts, see in general Abbot E. Smith, *Colonists in Bondage* (Chapel Hill, N.C., 1947), part II; for a close look at the processes involved and the latest estimate of overall figures, see the articles by A. Roger Ekirch and Kenneth Morgan in *W.M.Q.*, 42 (1985), 184–227.

25 *The Statutes at Large; Being a Collection of All the Laws of Virginia . . .*, ed. William W. Hening, II (New York, 1823), p. 510; William Stith, *The History of the First Discovery and Settlement of Virginia . . .* [1747], facsimile ed. (Spartanburg, S.C., 1965), p. 168; Hugh Jones, *The Present State of Virginia . . .* [1724], ed. Richard L. Morton (Chapel Hill, N.C., 1956), p. 135 (cf. pp. 87–88); William Livingston *et al.*, *The Independent Reflector . . .* [1752–1753], ed. Milton M. Klein (Cambridge, Mass., 1963), pp. 166, 165; Franklin's "Petition" to exchange American rattlesnakes for British convicts, in *Papers of Benjamin Franklin*, ed. Leonard W. Labaree *et al.* (New Haven, 1959–   ), XIII, 240–242.

26 Of the vast literature on New England Puritanism, Edmund Morgan's *Visible Saints: The History of a Puritan Idea* (New York, 1963) is crucial to this point. It traces out the New England Puritans' idea of the true church, based on earlier views but fully articulated and fulfilled only on these shores; it shaped all aspects of the Puritans' lives.

27 Two excellent articles have recently made the first serious entries into this fascinating and little-known subject: Jon Butler, "Magic, Astrology, and the Early American Religious Heritage, 1600–1760," *American Historical Review*, 84 (April 1979), 317–346; and Elizabeth W. Fisher, " 'Prophesies and Revelations': German Cabbalists in Early Pennsylvania," *Pennsylvania Magazine of History and Biography*, 109 (1985), 299–333. Butler concentrates on occultism and its relation to North American Protestantism; Fisher explores more generally the German background of the early Pennsylvania Pietists. For both, Johannes Kelpius is a key figure.

28 On Kelpius, see Julius F. Sachse's old and heavily documented but chaotic *The German Pietists of Provincial Pennsylvania* (Philadelphia, 1895), especially pp. 219–250, and the Butler and Fisher articles cited above. I have also used details in Ernest L. Lashlee, "Johannes Kelpius and His Woman in the Wilderness: A Chapter in the History of Colonial Pennsylvania Religious Thought," in *Glaube, Geist, Geschichte: Festschrift für Ernst Benz . . .*, ed. Gerhard Müller and Winfried Zeller (Leiden, 1967), 327–338.

29 Sachse, *German Pietists*, pp. 196, 335–340, 388–401.

30 The fullest account of Ephrata and its context is E. G. Alderfer, *The Ephrata Commune: An Early American Counterculture* (Pittsburgh, 1985), a sympathetic treatment which contains excellent sections on the German background and on the bizarre training Beissel's singers endured. They were fed special diets according to the parts they sang, practiced four hours at a time and then marched in a "spectral midnight procession," were dressed in sacramental white whenever they performed, and were instructed to sing with their heads declined but voices projected heavenward. Alderfer also summarizes well the extensive writing on Mann's use of Beissel in *Doctor Faustus*. The standard biography by Walter C. Klein, *Johann Conrad Beissel, Mystic and Martinet, 1690–1768*

(Philadelphia, 1942), is less sympathetic, and stresses the weird, rebarbative aspects of the *Vorsteher* and his cult. James E. Ernst, *Ephrata, A History* ([*Yearbook of*] *the Pennsylvania German Folklore Society*, XXV [1961], Philadelphia, 1963) brings out the importance of Beissel's Rosicrucianism and of the mystical rites practiced in Ephrata; and Julius F. Sachse's meandering *German Sectarians of Pennsylvania, 1708–1742: A Critical and Legendary History of the Ephrata Cloister and the Dunkers* (2 vols., Philadelphia, 1899) contains a wealth of information, some of it of dubious accuracy, and reproduces some of the key documents. For details on Beissel's singing school and a summary of his musical ideas, see Ernst, *Ephrata*, chap. 15; on his poetry (he wrote about 700 hymns), see Dennis McCort, "Johann Conrad Beissel, Colonial Mystic Poet," *German-American Studies*, 8 (Fall, 1974), 1–26.

Ephrata suited Voltaire's Enlightenment-propagandistic purposes perfectly, especially since the *philosophe* knew so little about the commune. In the article on the church in his *Philosophical Dictionary* (first printed separately, 1771) he called Ephrata a "secte des dunkards, ou des dumplers . . . espèce de religieux hospitaliers." *Oeuvres Complètes*, XVIII (*Dictionnaire Philosophique*, II), nouvelle éd. (Paris, 1878), 501: "elle [Beissel's sect] rejette le péché originel comme une impiété, et l'éternité des peines comme une barbarie. Leur vie pure ne leur laisse pas imaginer que Dieu puisse tourmenter ses créatures cruellement et éternellement. Égarés dans un coin du nouveau monde, loin du troupeau de l'Eglise catholique, ils sont jusqu'à présent, malgré cette malheureuse erreur, les plus justes et les plus inimitables des hommes."

31 Klein, *Beissel*, chaps. 3, 4, p. 100; Sachse, *German Sectarians*, I, 73–78; Gillian L. Gollin, *Moravians in Two Worlds* (New York, 1967); Jacob J. Sessler, *Communal Pietism among Early American Moravians* (New York, 1933); Hopple, "Spatial Development of the Southeastern Pennsylvania Plain Dutch Community to 1970," *Pennsylvania Folklife*, 21, no. 2 (1971–72), 18–20; 21, no. 3 (1972), 36–45.

32 "Report of the Journey of Francis Louis Michel from Berne, Switzerland, to Virginia [1701–1702]," *Virginia Magazine of History and Biography*, 24 (1916), 295; Milton W. Hamilton, *Sir William Johnson:*

Colonial American, 1715–1763 (Port Washington, N.Y., 1976), pp. 33–35, 304–305, 306–310; Lord Adam Gordon, "Journal of an Officer . . . in 1764 and 1765," in *Travels in the American Colonies,* ed. Newton D. Mereness (New York, 1916), p. 417.

33 Crane, *Southern Frontier,* chap. 5; James Axtell, "The White Indians of Colonial America," *W.M.Q.,* 32 (1975), 55–88; Vaughan and Richter, "Crossing the Cultural Divide," pp. 60–72; *Life, Letters and Papers of William Dunbar of Elgin, Morayshire, Scotland, and Natchez, Mississippi, Pioneer Scientist of the Southern United States,* ed. Eron Rowland (Jackson, Miss., 1930).

34 E. P. Panagopoulos, *New Smyrna: An Eighteenth Century Greek Odyssey* (Gainesville, Fla., 1966); Bailyn, *Voyagers,* chap. 12.

Index

Africa, emigration from:
  to Chesapeake colonies, 101–2
  magnitude of, 9
  to New York, 96
Amelia (Egmont) Island, 79
America, *see* North America
Amish settlements, 127
aristocracy, provincial, 66, 98–9
  homes of, 102–3

Baltimore, Lords, *see* Calvert
  family
barbarism, *see* savagery
Bartram, John, 75
Beissel, Johann Conrad, 125–7,
  165–6
"betterment migration," 23
birth and death rates:
  in Boston, 54
  in Chesapeake colonies, 100–1
  in New England, 93
  in Philadelphia, 56
Blackstone, William,
  Commentaries, 113–14
bonded servitude:
  in Chesapeake colonies, 100, 101

economic consequences of, 13
  in Maryland, 15
  and population growth, 13, 64,
  100
  and tobacco prices, 27–8
  see also servants, indentured
Boston:
  migration from, to country, 54
  population of, 53–5, 151
Bristol, England, 26
Britain:
  depopulation of, feared, 9–10,
  39, 73
  emigrants from, to America: in
  Chesapeake colonies, 99–100;
  convicts as, 61, 120–2, 164;
  destination patterns of, 15;
  family groups in, 11, 13;
  gender distribution of, 11;
  indentured servants as, *see*
  servants, indentured;
  metropolitan, 12–13, 15;
  number of, 5–6, 9–10, 40, 60;
  provincial, 13–15; Puritan,
  25–6; social characteristics of,
  11–15, 85–6

Index

Index

Index

Index

Index

A NOTE ON THE TYPE

This book was set in a digitized version of Janson. The hot-metal version of Janson was a recutting made direct from type cast from matrices long thought to have been made by the Dutchman Anton Janson, who was a practicing type founder in Leipzig during the years 1668–1687. However, it has been conclusively demonstrated that these types are actually the work of Nicholas Kis (1650–1702), a Hungarian, who most probably learned his trade from the master Dutch type founder Dirk Voskens. The type is an excellent example of the influential and sturdy Dutch types that prevailed in England up to the time William Caslon (1692–1766) developed his own imcomparable designs from them.

Composed, printed, and bound by the Haddon Craftsmen, Inc., Scranton, Pennsylvania. Designed by Betty Anderson.